Spelling Practice Workbook

Belongs To:

_____

Copyright © 2023 Newbee Publication

ALL RIGHTS RESERVED

This book may not be reproduced or transmitted in any form or by any means, electronic or mechanical, without written permission from the author.

Thanks for Purchase
Scan QR code for more publications

Word Cloud

remark, arctic, resist, continent, afford, diagram, rare, frail, capture, brief, grace, recognise, triumph, doze, habit, envy, accelerate, value, globe, hostile, response, threat, enable, journey, peculiar, advantage, deed, gasp, cling, limp, brave, impact, perform, coast, arena, shabby, wander, weary, attract, erupt, suitable, origin, blend, climate, glide, destruction, confess, vision, fragile, plunge, steer, brilliant, appeal, ordeal, swift, observe, custom

venture, reduce, descend, coax, valiant, border, prevent, essential, mystify, fortunate, abrupt, active, avoid, struggle, adopt, anticipate, scatter, prepare, extend, passage, responsible, rely, grasp, former, abundant, mock, humble, abandon, ancestor, loyal, fierce, alert, deposit, coward, tragic, inspire, release, contain, represent, respect, desire, explore, variety, advice, risk, balance, orchard, instant, content, bounce, examine, terror, convince, dense, ancient, launch

How to use this Spelling Workbook

If you're looking to improve your spelling skills, this practice workbook is a great resource. The first lesson includes instructions and examples, and you'll find word search solutions at the end of the book. To make the most of your practice time, here are some tips to keep in mind:

- Only practice when you're feeling focused and ready to learn.
- Take your time with each exercise and avoid trying to complete the entire workbook in one sitting.
- Use a dictionary to look up word meanings rather than using digital tools.
- Keep track of any words you struggle with and make a point of practicing them more frequently.
- Try incorporating new words into your writing and speech to help reinforce your learning.
- Regularly review the words you've learned to help cement them in your long-term memory.
- Don't hesitate to ask for help if you're having difficulty with a particular word or concept.
- Lastly, celebrate your progress and accomplishments along the way to help keep yourself motivated and engaged.
- You can photocopy pages to practice again or consider purchasing part 2 of the workbook once you've finished.

Lesson 1

Re-write Words

Active			
Observe			
Cling			
Convince			
Extend			
Struggle			

Find Letters

Active	g (a) p s (c) n o d m j a (t) p e l w p (i) s o (v) h n p i (e)
Observe	g r o j n b A m q c l b p c t s u w r o j a v t e k n
Cling	z a m b c e q a n h d s r u e i b r m k e a j t w i
Convince	L k j i a l n d m c s h k i o q e t d v x y e h g d n
Extend	A b d l b d g i a l p t r n g h t q x e f l n c j k t y p
struggle	B p s e m k l q o n e f j c d i h a u r t d l e p w b

Find Meanings from Dictionary and write them here

Active _____

Observe _____

Cling _____

Convince _____

Extend _____

Struggle _____

Write out these words in Capital letters

active _____

observe _____

cling _____

convince _____

extend _____

struggle _____

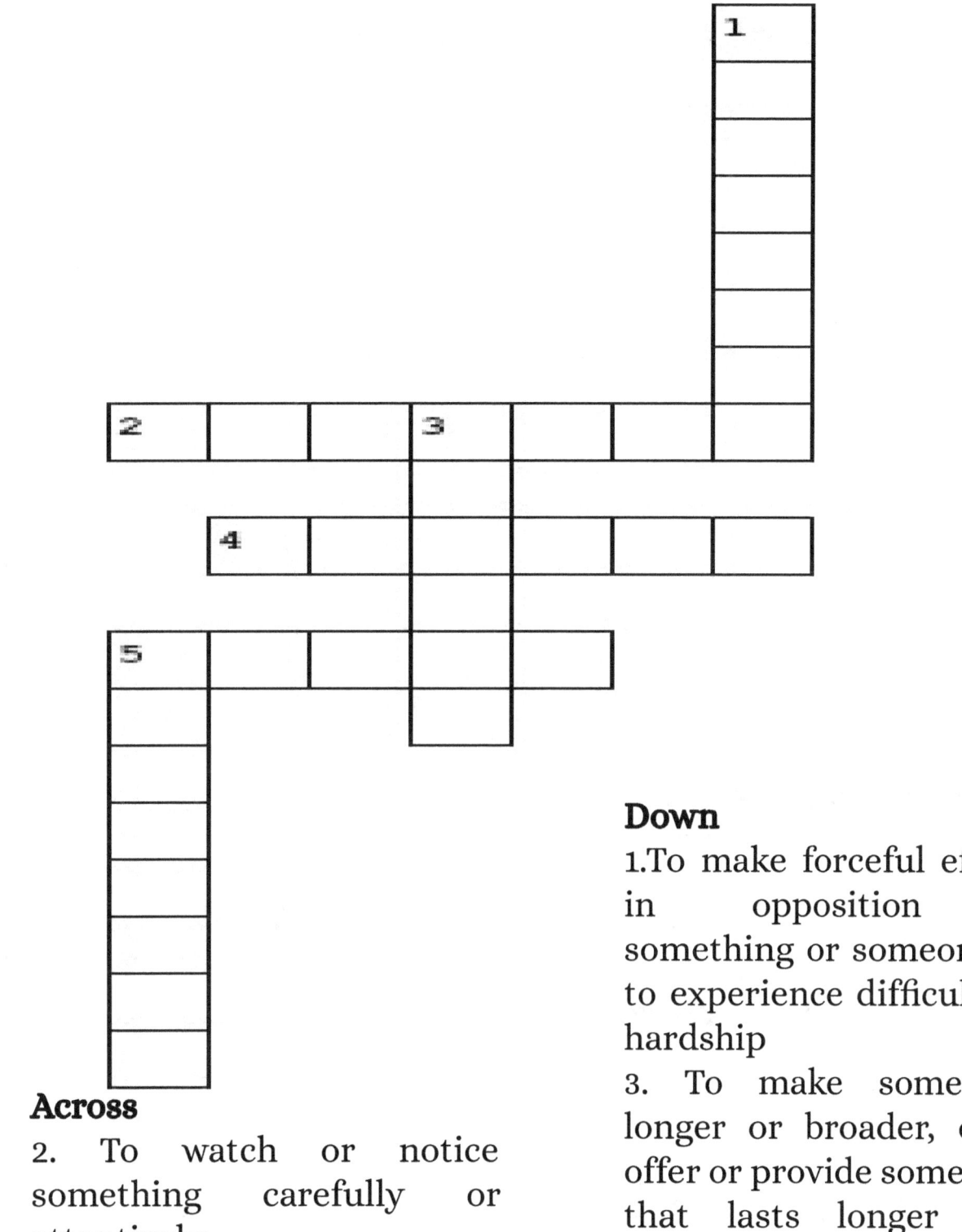

Across
2. To watch or notice something carefully or attentively.
4. Engaged in action or involved in ongoing activity.
5. To hold onto something tightly or persistently, as if afraid to let go.

Down
1. To make forceful efforts in opposition to something or someone, or to experience difficulty or hardship
3. To make something longer or broader, or to offer or provide something that lasts longer than expected.
5. To persuade someone to believe or do something through reasoning or argument.

Write out the Synonyms and Antonyms of these words

	Synonyms	Antonyms
Active		
Observe		
Cling		
Convince		
Extend		
Struggle		

Match the Unscramble Words

Active	geslturg	....struggle......
Oserve	entxed	....
Cling	viteea	....
Convince	gincl	....
Extend	ovrebse	....
Struggle	nceiovnc	....

Fill the blanks and Make the sentences using above words

1. The athlete was very _____ during the game, running and jumping all over the field.
2. If you take a moment to _____ your surroundings, you might notice some interesting details.
3. The baby monkey likes to _____ to its mother's back as she swings through the trees.
4. It can be difficult to _____ someone to change their opinion, especially if they feel strongly about it.
5. The company decided to _____ the deadline for the project to give the team more time to work on it.
6. Despite his _____ with the difficult math problem, the student persevered and eventually found the solution.

Match the words to the shape

Active, Observe, Cling, Convince, Extend, Struggle

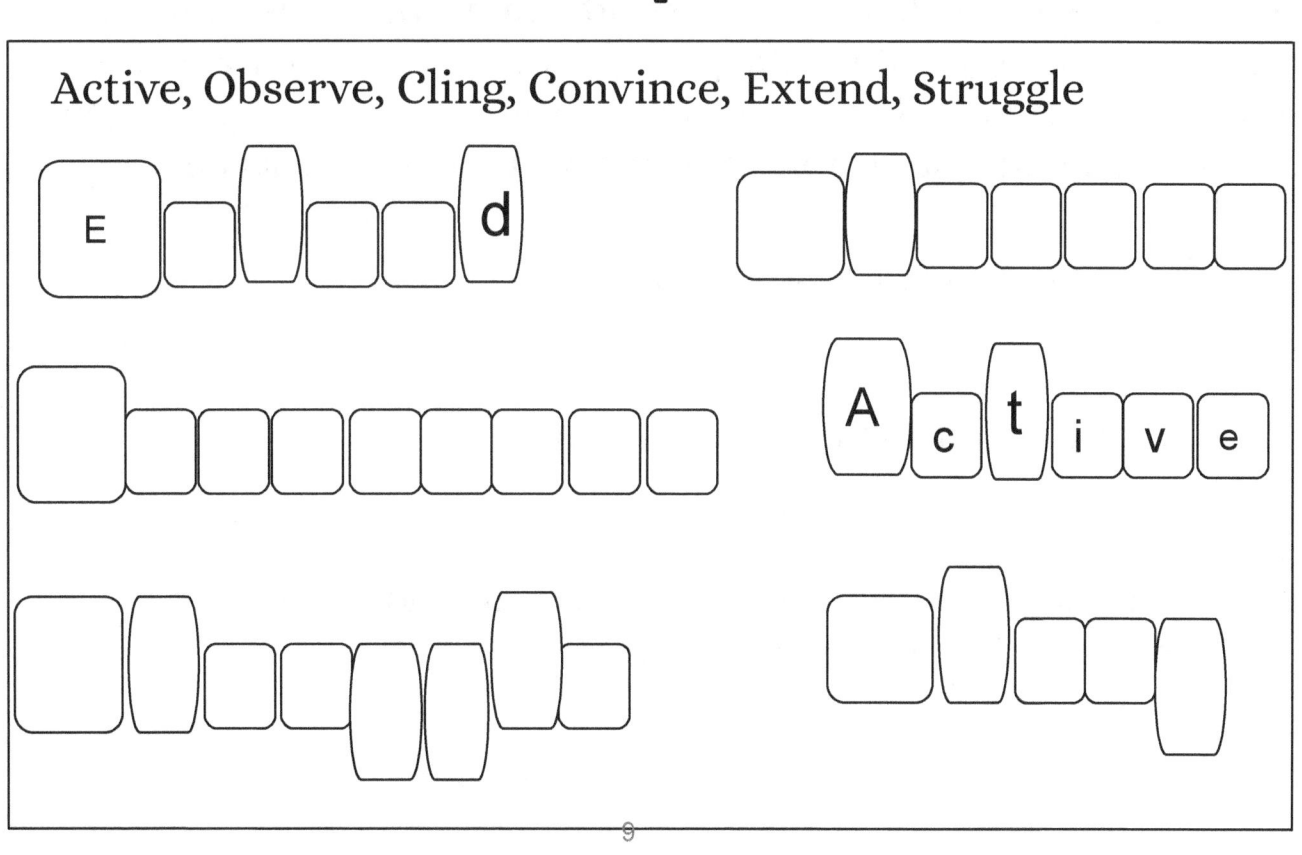

Reading Comprehension
Read the story: underline the words you have learned in this lesson and answer the questions

Lena was always an active person. She loved to hike, bike, and swim, and always made time for these activities in her busy schedule. One day, while on a hike, she stopped to observe a group of birds flying overhead. She marveled at their grace and precision, and made a mental note to learn more about birdwatching.

As she continued on her hike, Lena came across a steep and rocky trail. She struggled to find her footing, but refused to give up. She clung to the rocks, inching her way up the trail until she finally made it to the top. Exhausted but proud, she extended her arms out wide and took in the stunning view.

Later that week, Lena had a difficult conversation with a friend who had different opinions about a topic. She used her communication skills to listen to her friend's perspective and share her own, ultimately convincing her friend to see things in a new light.

The experience made Lena realize how important it is to be active not just physically, but mentally and emotionally as well. She learned that by observing, clinging to what matters, convincing others, and extending herself, she could grow and overcome any challenge.

1. What activities did Lena enjoy?

2. What did Lena observe on her hike?

3. What did Lena learn about communication from her conversation with her friend?

Lesson 1

Y	Y	X	T	W	A	E	Y	I	O	H	F	O	L	Q	P
O	S	V	T	L	J	N	D	G	N	K	Y	X	N	W	L
Z	X	T	J	S	F	L	L	K	R	O	I	P	J	B	I
N	W	Q	R	D	K	J	H	S	C	P	I	O	I	P	F
E	I	R	Z	U	J	O	S	Q	V	L	R	I	R	X	K
E	W	V	M	I	G	B	M	D	C	D	K	Q	F	R	J
W	X	N	S	J	Z	G	U	S	O	C	L	I	N	G	H
O	N	T	R	O	D	B	L	A	N	T	M	R	W	B	W
B	N	Z	E	E	D	J	F	E	V	A	J	Q	R	T	F
P	B	O	P	N	I	Z	E	G	I	C	H	C	K	F	O
W	G	Y	U	Z	D	V	A	F	N	T	F	E	V	H	V
K	R	T	A	X	R	Z	Y	O	C	I	E	F	R	R	I
J	I	G	F	E	F	J	O	M	E	V	J	J	O	D	S
L	S	Q	S	H	E	O	N	C	J	E	L	Q	Y	T	O
G	P	B	M	B	R	Z	D	E	Q	T	Q	Q	L	E	G
H	O	T	F	Z	V	Z	W	B	H	K	N	P	R	N	Z

ACTIVE
CONVINCE
OBSERVE

CLING
EXTEND
STRUGGLE

What rhymes with these words

Active —— Acting, action....

Observe ——

Cling —— Sling, sing, sting, ding.....

Convince ——

Extend ——

Struggle ——

Find hidden words

Active —— Act, vice, Cave...

Observe ——

Cling ——

Convince ——

Extend ——

Struggle ——

Lesson 2

Re-write Words

Arctic			
Border			
Climate			
Fierce			
Mystify			
Steer			

Find Letters

Arctic	g a p s r n o d c m j a t p e l w p i s o v h c p i
Border	g r o j n b A m q c l b p c t s u w r o j a v t e k n
Climate	z a m b c e q a n h d s r u e i b r m k e a j t w i
Fierce	L k j i a l n d m c s h k i o q e t d v x y e h g d n
Mystify	A b d l b d g i a l p t r n g h t q x e f l n c j k t y p
Steer	B p s e m k l q o n e f j c d i h a u r t d l e p w b

Find Meanings from Dictionary and write them here

Arctic _____

Border _____

Climate _____

Fierce _____

Mystify _____

Steer _____

Write out these words in Capital letters

arctic _____

border _____

climate _____

fierce _____

mystify _____

steer _____

Lesson 2

Across
5. To guide or direct a vehicle, vessel, or animal in a particular direction.
6. The long-term atmospheric conditions of a region, including temperature, humidity, and precipitation.

Down
1. Intense, powerful, and aggressive in nature.
2. Pertaining to the region around the North Pole.
3. To confuse or puzzle someone by being difficult to understand or explain.
4. The line or frontier area separates two countries or territories

Write out the Synonyms and Antonyms of these words

	Synonyms	Antonyms
Arctic		
Border		
Climate		
Fierce		
Mystify		
Steer		

Match the Unscramble Words

Arctic	telamic	....
Border	efreic	....
Climate	erets	....
Fierce	triacc	....
Mystify	drbroe	....
Steer	sfyitym	....

Fill the blanks and Make the sentences using above words

1. A _ _ _ _ _ region characterized by cold temperatures and polar ice.
2. The line separating two countries or areas; a _ _ _ _ _ .
3. The prevailing weather patterns and conditions of a region; the _ _ _ _ _ _ _ of an area.
4. The lion's _____ roar could be heard throughout the jungle.
5. The magician's tricks _____ the audience, leaving them wondering how he did it.
6. Tom need to _____ the boat to the left in order to avoid the rocks.

Match the words to the shape

Arctic, Border, Climate, Fierce, Mystify, Steer

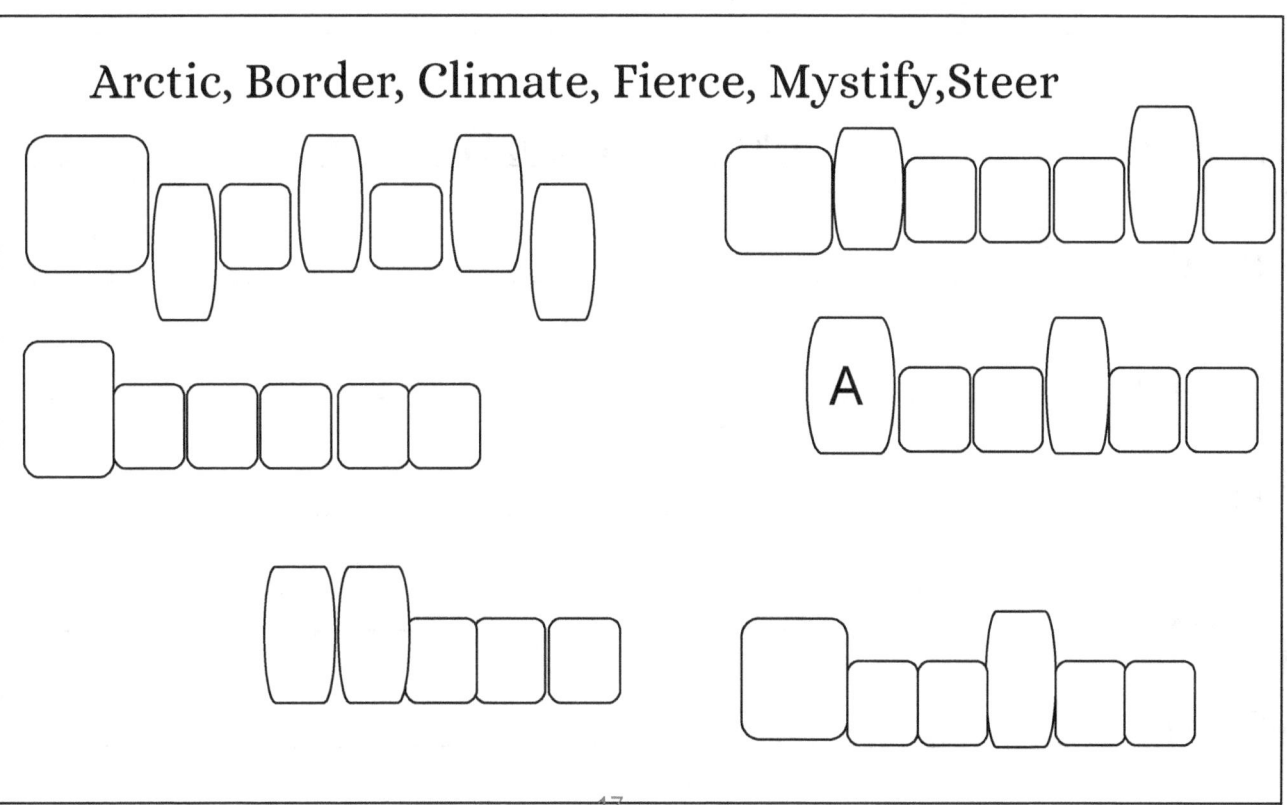

What rhymes with these words

Arctic — Artic, arotic, hectic, lactic....

Border — Hortor, mortar, ardor, carder....

Climate —

Fierce —

Mystify —

Steer —

Find hidden words

Arctic — Arc, cacti, cart.....

Border —

Climate —

Fierce —

Mystify —

Steer —

Write a Story using the words you have learned in this lesson

Lesson 2

```
m k r r h a s p y v g i q c i o
o j y e x g q f i o r m f e i o
l y r n t a d u p e z d d b s i
o l h e e a j e e o h t l c i k
j c l b d x m t i j h v s b w z
w v h g h p s i q t m w l o m x
j y o k f z c u l d v u r v r
e b f o m i u h k c z o l d w j
w r y i e c g i d r z h q e c m
s k f q t z i o u l y w z r n z
c n d g z s t z c z f m p d e c
i q z b a b y u q i w u c q q i
t o a c i i k m e m l v q v v p
c r u r i a g r b i q g j q g r
r q y y u p c t j c e r g j t j
a s e j p e x j w n a a b x s h
```

ARCTIC BORDER
CLIMATE
FIERCE MYSTIFY
STEER

Lesson 3

Re-write Words

Afford			
Confess			
Reduce			
Prepare			
Terror			
Ordeal			

Find Letters

Afford	g a p s c n o f m j a f p e l o p i s r v h n p d e
Confess	g r o c n b A m q o l b p n t s f w r e j a s t e k s
Reduce	r a m b c e q a n h d s r u e i b r c k e a j t w i e
Prepare	L p j i a l r d m e s h k i p q e a d v r y e h g d n
Terror	A b t l b d g e a l p t r n g r t q x o f l n c r k t y
Ordeal	B p s e o k l q o n r f j c d i h e a u r t d l e p w b

Find Meanings from Dictionary and write them here

Afford _____

Confess _____

Reduce _____

Prepare _____

Terror _____

Ordeal _____

Write out these words in Capital letters

afford _____

confess _____

reduce _____

prepare _____

terror _____

ordeal _____

Write out the Synonyms and Antonyms of these words

	Synonyms	Antonyms
Afford		
Confess		
Prepare		
Reduce		
Terror		
Ordeal		

Match the Unscramble Words

Afford   rladeo   _____

Confess   erortr   _____

Prepare   deucre   _____

Ordeal   rffaro   _____

Reduce   ofecssn   _____

Terror   aprepre   _____

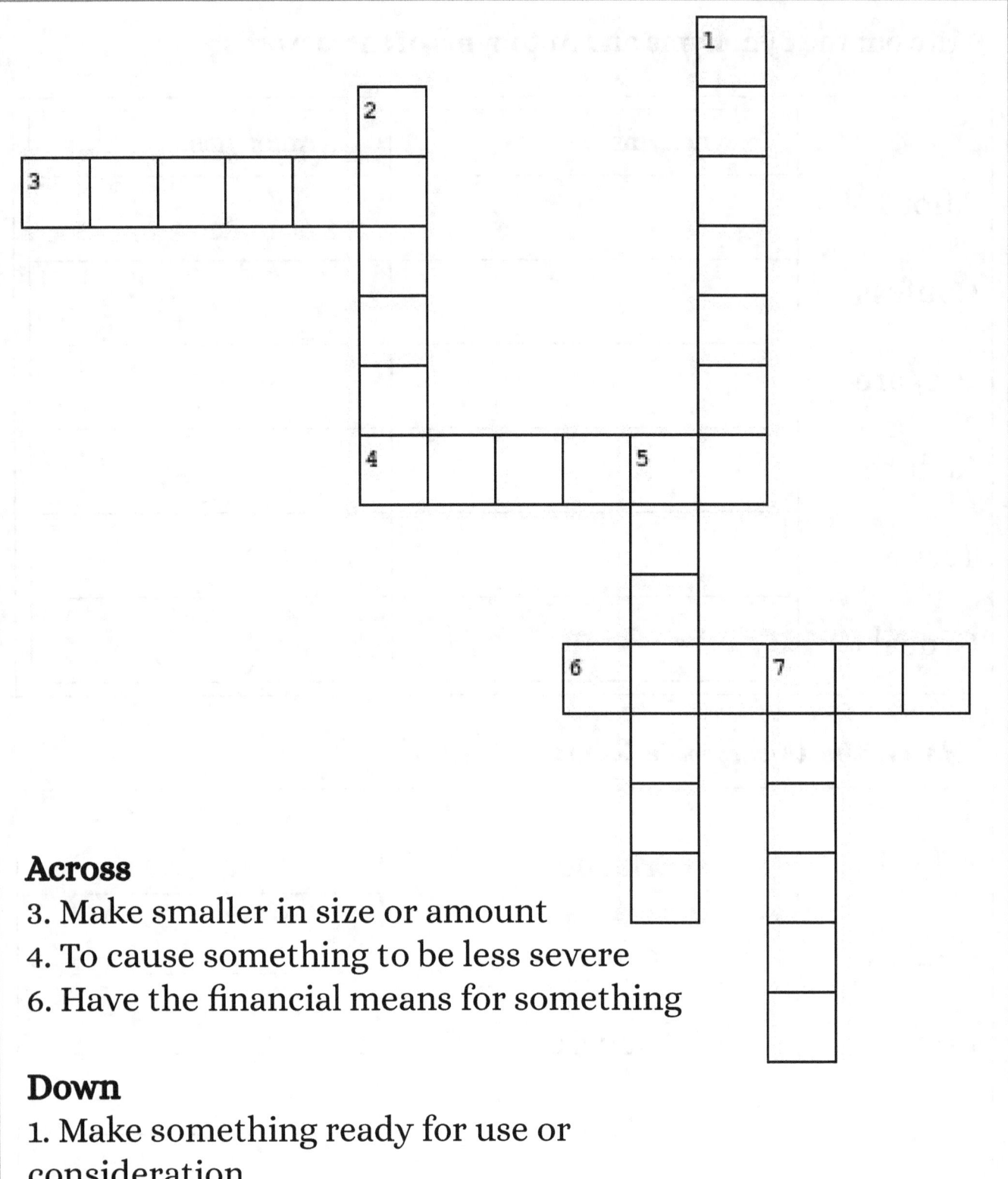

Across

3. Make smaller in size or amount
4. To cause something to be less severe
6. Have the financial means for something

Down

1. Make something ready for use or consideration
2. Extreme fear
5. Admit to wrongdoing
7. Difficult or painful experience

Fill the blanks and Make the sentences using above words

1. I really can't _____ to buy a new car right now.
2. It took a lot of courage to _____ my true feelings to my best friend.
3. I need to _____ some food before the guests arrive.
4. If you want to lose weight, you should_____ your calorie intake.
5. The _____ of the earthquake left the city in ruins.
6. Going through a breakup can be a difficult _____ to deal with.

Match the words to the shape

Afford, Confess, Prepare, Reduce, Terror, Ordeal

Lesson 3

```
o k k n b j e m m k k z i l r q
p d a l y f r h i l w i c o n y
k q y c r w a n l v x e o n y c
b t t k e d p o u j x q n m m j
n k e f d e e y k b a o f m y d
f h r a u f r v u r q f e c s y
s c r q c x p n f q o i s k y n
l n o p e w v t u a q x s q w p
k v r t k c a b l f i r r t p h
v e i e w r d o f c h h p j y r
o m e o e r d q s d e g k o p r
r h k q v w u y a k b w r b n
n l o m h c d r o f f a p d e j
c t p h s y h f c p k i g e e r
j k i a t l p p l l e e h a r c
p p m f z a t c d d m e x l k l
```

AFFORD CONFESS
ORDEAL PREPARE
REDUCE TERROR

What rhymes with these words

Afford   _____

Confess   _____

Reduce   _____

Prepare   _____

Terror   _____

Ordeal   _____

Find hidden words

Afford   _____

Confess   _____

Reduce   _____

Prepare   _____

Terror   _____

Ordeal   _____

Lesson 4

Re-write Words

Capture			
Fortunate			
Adopt			
Advantage			
Frail			
Origin			

Find Letters

Capture	g a p s c n o d m j a t p e t w p u s o r h n p i e
Fortunate	g r o f n b A m q o l r p c t s u w r n j a v t e k n
Adopt	z a m b c e q a n h d s r u e o b r m p e a j t w i
Advantage	L k j i a l n d m c v h k i a q n t d a x y u h g d e
Frail	A b d l f d g i a l p t r n g h a q x i f l n c j k t y p
Origin	B p o e m k l q r n e f i c d g h a u i t d l n p w b

Find Meanings from Dictionary and write them here

Capture _____

Fortunate _____

Adopt _____

Advantage _____

Frail _____

Origin _____

Write out these words in Capital letters

capture _____

fortunate _____

adopt _____

advantage _____

frail _____

origin _____

Fill the blanks and Make the sentences using above words

1. After the long hike, she was feeling _____ and needed to rest for a while.
2. His talent and hard work gave him an _____ over his competitors in the job market.
3. The young couple decided to _____ a child from a foreign country and give them a loving home.
4. Learning a foreign language can be a great _____ for traveling and communicating with people from other cultures.
5. The _____ of the mysterious artifact was finally revealed after years of research and study.
6. Winning the scholarship was a _____ opportunity that allowed her to pursue her dream of higher education.

Match the words to the shape

Capture, Fortunate, Adopt, Advantage, Frail, Origin

Write out the Synonyms and Antonyms of these words

	Synonyms	Antonyms
Capture		
Fortunate		
Adopt		
Advantage		
Frail		
Origin		

Match the Unscramble Words

Capture	taevangad	------------------------------
Fortunate	rioign	------------------------------
Adopt	uantrtefo	------------------------------
Advantage	etaucrp	------------------------------
Frail	aotdp	------------------------------
Origin	irlfa	------------------------------

Across
3. Lucky or favoured by circumstances or events.
5. To take possession or control of something, often through force or strategy.
6. Physically weak or delicate, often due to age or illness.

Down
1. The point or place where something begins, arises, or is derived from.
2. To legally take on the responsibility of raising and caring for a child or animal that is not biologically one's own.
4. A favourable or superior circumstance or position that gives one a greater chance of success or victory.

What rhymes with these words

capture   _____

fortunate   _____

adopt   _____

advantage   _____

frail   _____

origin   _____

Find hidden words

capture   _____

fortunate   _____

adopt   _____

advantage   _____

frail   _____

origin   _____

Lesson 4

y	t	b	j	e	g	t	b	o	m	u	w	p	h	h	o
l	b	e	s	z	p	a	w	v	e	z	e	h	c	l	y
i	p	e	s	o	r	q	e	f	x	q	g	u	v	j	m
b	n	g	d	k	l	q	u	r	o	a	u	v	u	g	q
e	c	a	p	t	u	r	e	b	m	p	w	s	h	e	o
f	x	k	r	o	m	e	s	h	e	s	u	r	t	f	v
m	o	y	v	v	t	y	h	g	j	f	i	l	g	n	l
w	w	r	f	e	a	k	a	k	w	l	r	g	y	l	i
r	o	v	t	n	w	t	w	t	a	j	z	a	n	i	u
v	t	r	g	u	n	u	f	x	y	k	f	t	i	d	x
a	q	z	i	a	n	g	n	k	v	x	w	h	v	l	x
s	x	w	v	g	v	a	h	t	l	n	j	f	z	p	y
u	y	d	o	k	i	h	t	v	q	h	o	k	t	n	r
b	a	s	d	u	w	n	b	e	p	c	l	h	e	e	x
t	k	m	a	v	t	z	i	i	a	c	v	z	w	v	u
d	b	y	o	y	w	s	w	u	b	j	r	k	w	u	r

adopt
capture
frail

advantage
fortunate
origin

Lesson 5

Re-write Words

Perform			
Scatter			
Balance			
Advice			
Plunge			
Swift			

Find Letters

Perform	g a p s c e n r d m j a f p e t w p u s o r h n m p
Scatter	g r o f s b A c q a l r p c t s u t w e n j a r t e k n
Balance	z a m b c e q a n h l s r u a o b r n p c a j t w e
Advice	L k j i a l n d m c v h k i a q n t d c x y u h g d e
Plunge	A b d l p d g i a l p t r n g h u q x i f l n c j g t e p
Swift	B p s e m k l w r n e f i c d g f a u i t d l n p w b

Across

3. Recommendations or suggestions given to someone (Hint: synonym of guidance)

5. To execute a task or action with skill and precision (Hint: synonym of carry out)

Down

1. The state of being evenly distributed or having stability (Hint: opposite of imbalance)

2. To spread or throw things in different directions (Hint: rhymes with matter)

4. Move quickly and with great _____ (Hint: rhymes with drift)

5. To jump or dive into something quickly and without hesitation (Hint: synonym of dive)

Find Meanings from Dictionary and write them here

Perform _____

Scatter _____

Balance _____

Advice _____

Plunge _____

Swift _____

Write out these words in Capital letters

Perform _____

Scatter _____

Balance _____

Advice _____

Plunge _____

Swift _____

Write out the Synonyms and Antonyms of these words

	Synonyms	Antonyms
Perform		
Scatter		
Balance		
Advice		
Plunge		
Swift		

Match the Unscramble Words

Perform	uenpgl	------------------------------
Scatter	avcedi	------------------------------
Balance	mrpofre	------------------------------
Advice	tfiws	------------------------------
Plunge	alcabne	------------------------------
Swift	ecrtast	------------------------------

Reading Comprehension
Read the story: underline the words you have learned in this lesson

Mark was a young musician with a passion for performing. He had been practicing for weeks in preparation for his first big gig, but as he took the stage, he felt his nerves begin to scatter. He closed his eyes and took a deep breath, trying to balance his nerves with his excitement.

As he began to play, Mark felt himself getting lost in the music. His fingers moved with swift precision across the keys, and his heart soared with every note. But just as he hit the climax of his performance, he made a mistake and hit the wrong note. Mark felt his heart plunge as he realized his mistake.

After the show, Mark's mentor came up to him with some advice. "You're a talented musician," she said, "but you need to find your balance. You can't let your nerves get the best of you, or you'll never perform to your full potential."

Mark took her advice to heart and began practicing mindfulness and meditation to help calm his nerves. He also sought out opportunities to perform in smaller venues to help build his confidence.

Eventually, Mark was offered another big gig. This time, he felt more prepared and balanced than ever before. He took the stage with a calm confidence and gave a flawless performance that left the audience in awe.

From that day on, Mark made it his mission to help other young musicians find their balance and overcome their nerves. He scattered the seeds of advice wherever he went, and watched as they took root and flourished.

Fill the blanks and Make the sentences using above words

1. _____ action is needed to _____ the emergency procedure.

2. It's important to _____ seeds evenly to ensure proper growth.

3. Finding a _____ between work and personal life can improve overall well-being.

4. Seeking _____ from a mentor can help navigate difficult career decisions.

5. Sometimes, it's necessary to take a _____ and try something new.

Match the words to the shape

Perform, Scatter, Balance, Advice, Plunge, Swift

Lesson 5

e	w	t	y	b	e	i	d	e	v	s	w	d	r	s
h	z	o	r	o	t	d	k	e	k	l	h	t	q	y
n	p	m	d	o	c	k	x	s	v	a	h	i	t	a
t	a	d	l	p	x	h	r	g	f	u	s	o	o	f
j	j	s	o	i	e	p	w	j	c	p	w	a	n	e
e	n	z	c	z	x	i	f	j	j	f	k	f	m	r
n	y	k	t	a	j	k	d	k	p	f	h	g	o	f
r	g	f	n	a	t	q	h	u	i	x	t	x	j	o
u	l	j	k	q	d	t	p	l	u	n	g	e	z	r
y	y	j	u	f	v	v	e	s	a	t	w	i	q	m
z	l	z	o	x	w	z	b	r	r	u	z	u	d	v
f	q	g	l	u	a	i	k	j	h	k	e	e	j	r
r	n	g	f	z	k	a	j	o	a	c	l	y	u	i
g	j	j	b	b	a	l	a	n	c	e	u	d	i	w
o	e	a	i	u	y	j	g	m	a	d	v	i	c	c
z	i	u	b	t	x	u	y	z	t	m	w	h	l	o

ADVICE
PERFORM
SCATTER

BALANCE
PLUNGE
SWIFT

What rhymes with these words

Perform _____

Scatter _____

Balance _____

Advice _____

Plunge _____

Swift _____

Find hidden words

Perform _____

Scatter _____

Balance _____

Advice _____

Plunge _____

Swift _____

Lesson 6

Re-write Words

Ancient			
Abandon			
Contain			
Launch			
Passage			
Grasp			

Find Letters

Ancient	g a p s c e n r c m j i f p e t w p n s o r t n m p i
Abandon	g r o f s b A c q a b r p a t s n t w e d j a o t k n
Contain	z a m b c e q a n h o s r u n o b t n p c a j t i e n
Launch	L k j i a l n d m c a h k i u q n t d c x y u h g d e
Passage	A b d l p d g i a l p t s n g h s q x a f l n c j g t e i
Grasp	B p s e m g l w r n e f i a d g f u i t d l n p w b n

Find Meanings from Dictionary and write them here

Ancient _____

Abandon _____

Contain _____

Launch   _____

Passage _____

Grasp   _____

Write out these words in Capital letters

ancient _____

abandon _____

contain _____

launch   _____

passage _____

grasp   _____

Complete following passage with the words you are practicing in this lesson

The archaeologists were thrilled to have discovered a new site with evidence of an _____ civilization. They carefully sifted through the soil to _____ artifacts that had been left behind by the people who once lived there. As they dug deeper, they found a sealed chamber that appeared to _____ something of great importance. With careful precision, they cracked open the container to reveal a map that showed the location of a hidden _____ site. The team immediately made plans to _____ an expedition to explore the new discovery, but first they had to navigate the treacherous _____ through the mountains to reach their destination. Despite the challenges, they were determined to _____ this opportunity to uncover the secrets of the past.

Match the words to the shape

Ancient, Abandon, Contain, Launch, Passage, Grasp

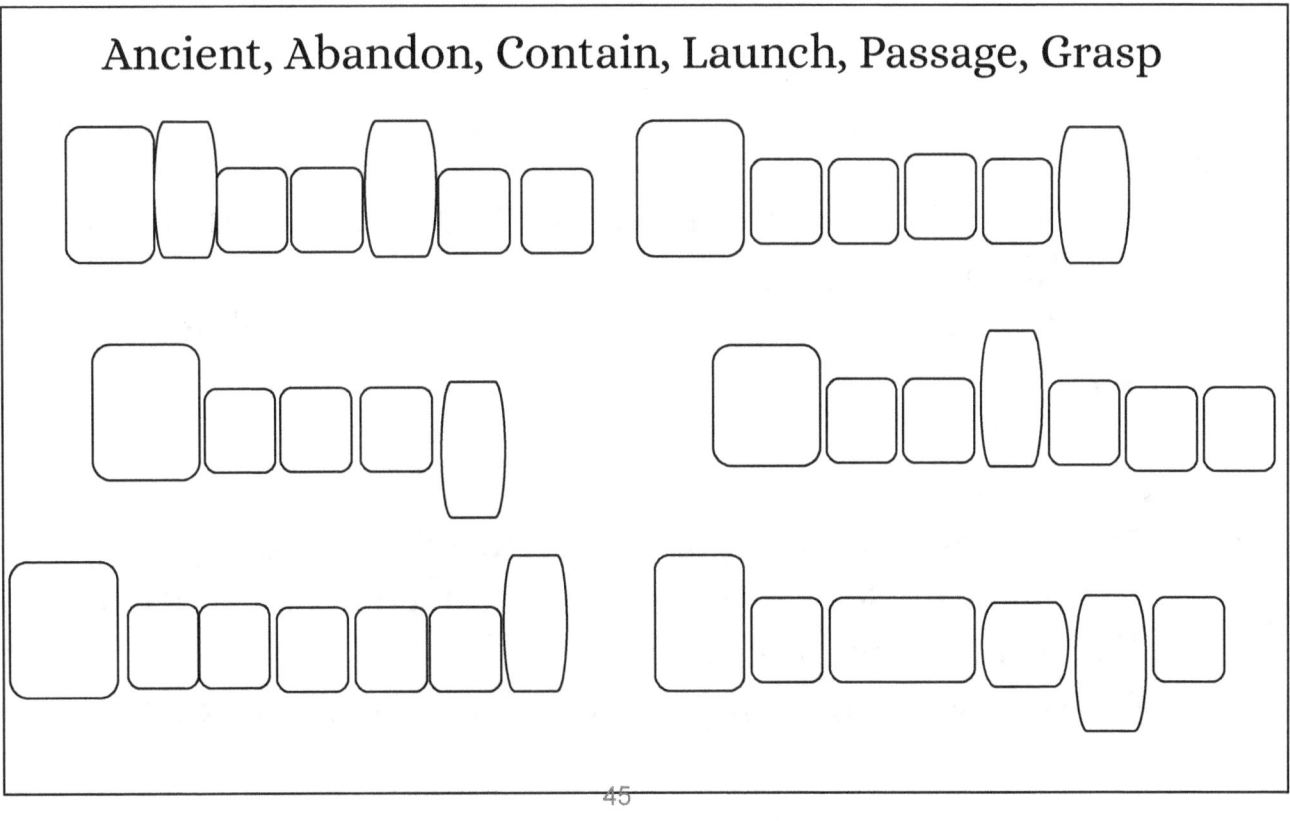

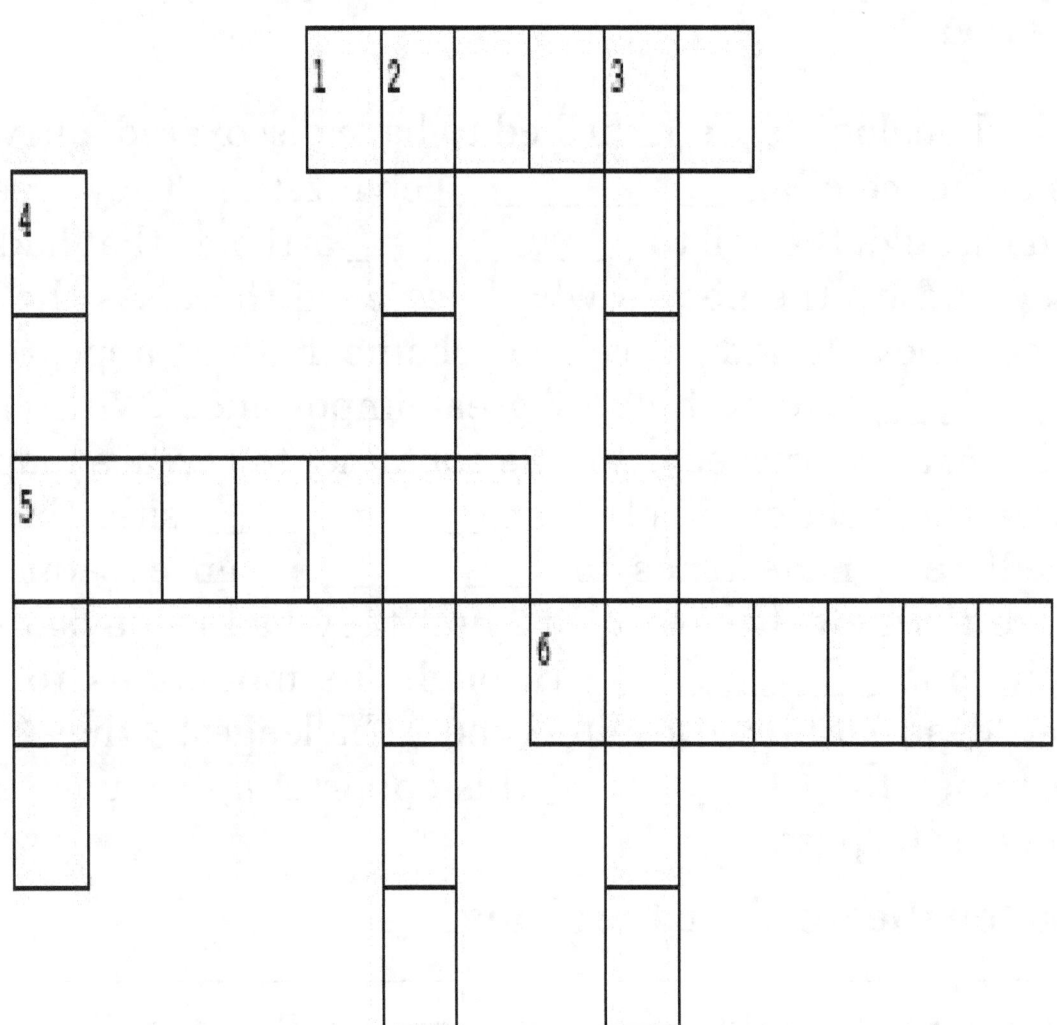

Across
1. To start or begin something, like a rocket or a business.
5. Old, historic, or _____.
6. A narrow way through something, like a tunnel or a channel.

Down
2. To let go of something or someone, often abruptly.
3. To hold or enclose something within a defined space or area, like a container or a garden.
4. To hold onto something tightly, like a rope or a concept.

Write out the Synonyms and Antonyms of these words

	Synonyms	Antonyms
Ancient		
Abandon		
Contain		
Launch		
Passage		
Grasp		

Match the Unscramble Words

Ancient	naluhc	------------------
Abandon	asspeag	------------------
Contain	prags	------------------
Launch	obnadna	------------------
Passage	cnnaeit	------------------
Grasp	taocnin	------------------

What rhymes with these words

Ancient _____

Abandon _____

Contain _____

Launch _____

Passage _____

Grasp _____

Find hidden words

Ancient _____

Abandon _____

Contain _____

Launch _____

Passage _____

Grasp _____

Identify the synonyms and antonyms of the words you are practicing in this lesson by circling them.

Synonyms:
The team of archaeologists was (elated) to have discovered a new site with evidence of a time-honored civilization. They meticulously sorted through the soil to seize artifacts that had been left behind by the people who once lived there. As they excavated further, they uncovered a sealed chamber that seemed to confine something of great importance. With precise care, they opened the container to disclose a map that indicated the whereabouts of a concealed takeoff site. The team promptly made arrangements to commence an expedition to explore the new discovery, but first they had to traverse the hazardous corridor through the mountains to reach their destination. Despite the challenges, they were determined to embrace this opportunity to uncover the secrets of the past.

Antonyms:
The squad of modern-day explorers was crestfallen to have uncovered a recent site with proof of a new civilization. They carelessly rummaged through the soil to abandon artifacts that had been left behind by the people who once lived there. As they destroyed further, they revealed an unsealed chamber that seemed to release something of little importance. With careless disregard, they broke open the container to conceal a map that obscured the whereabouts of a visible landing site. The team reluctantly made plans to conclude an expedition to neglect the new discovery, but first, they had to circumvent the manageable corridor through the mountains to reach their destination. Despite the ease, they were unenthusiastic to relinquish this opportunity to uncover the secrets of the present.

Lesson 6

```
t k j b p g b f p l x l y i t x
y x z w f o q e z c e t i b b p
s j g m z c g o o m i w h v s v
x n r h o s b v s p t e g l h p
u r y z n h i b o b e n s w o o
p t a n c i e n t s j g g r o d
a y f k l a u n c h n m n e z n
e r j s f e c o n t a i n z j x
q b r j w i j l g r a s p r f b
j a o a a q x j n n x f u e r k
n b l j r t p a s s a g e h n a
o p z b b q f s p q t l z k m z
u e i j k f u e e o w o m s r d
y s i a l s u m v s m x g k m o
n o i j v c t e a b a n d o n h
r k z s b m h g x n o p z e u y
```

ABANDON   ANCIENT
CONTAIN   GRASP
LAUNCH   PASSAGE

Lesson 7

Re-write Words

Gasp			
Abundant			
Enable			
Triumph			
Rely			
Risk			

Find Letters

Gasp	g a p s c e n r c m j i f p e t w p n s o r t n m p i
Abundant	g r o f s b A c q a b r p u t s n t d e d j a o n k t
Enable	z a m b c e q a n h o s r a n o b t n p l a j t i e n
Triumph	t k j i r l n d m c a h k i u q m t d c x p u h g d e
Rely	A b d l p d r i a l p t e n g h s q x a f l n c j y t e i
Risk	B p s e m g l w r n e f i a d g f u s t d l n k w b n

Find Meanings from Dictionary and write them here

Gasp _____

Abundant _____

Enable _____

Triumph _____

Rely _____

Risk _____

Write out these words in Capital letters

gasp _____

abundant _____

enable _____

triumph _____

rely _____

risk _____

Fill this passage by using words you are practicing in this lesson

As I stood at the edge of the cliff, I couldn't help but _____ at the breathtaking view. The clear blue sky stretched out as far as the eye could see, with the sun slowly setting in the distance. The sound of crashing waves below added to the sense of awe and wonder I felt.

I took a deep breath, letting the _____ air fill my lungs, and felt a surge of adrenaline rush through my body. It was time to take a leap of faith, to trust in myself and in the equipment that would _____ me to fly.

With a running start, I launched myself off the cliff and felt the wind rush past me as I soared through the air. It was a moment of pure _____ - the sense of freedom and joy I experienced was indescribable.

As I landed safely on the beach below, I couldn't help but feel grateful for the people I could _____ on to make my dreams a reality. It was only with their support and guidance that I was able to take the _____ of flying and turn it into a reality.

Across
4. A large amount or quantity
6. To fail or suffer a defeat (Antonym of Triumph)
7. To prevent or make it difficult for someone to do something (Antonym of Enable)
8. To depend on or have faith in someone or something

Down
1. Scanty or inadequate (Antonym of Abundant)
2. A feeling of surprise or shock
3. To give someone the ability or means to do something
5. A great victory or success
8. The possibility of something bad happening

Write out the Synonyms and Antonyms of these words

	Synonyms	Antonyms
Gasp		
Abundant		
Enable		
Triumph		
Rely		
Risk		

Match the Unscramble Words

Gasp	uirhptm	----------------
Abundant	sikr	----------------
Enable	pags	----------------
Triumph	natubdna	----------------
Rely	nlaeeb	----------------
Risk	lrye	----------------

Underline the antonyms of words you have learned

1. Rather than gasping in surprise, she let out a relaxed sigh when she saw her old friend.
2. The jungle was rich and lush, with an abundant amount of plant life, unlike the barren and empty desert.
3. The computer program disabled her ability to manually make changes, but it enabled her to work more efficiently.
4. Instead of triumphing over her opponent, she graciously accepted her defeat with a smile.
5. He distrusted himself and was unable to rely on his own judgment, always seeking advice from others.
6. Being overly cautious and never taking risks prevented him from reaching his full potential.
7. The community was very mindful and frugal, conserving resources and using them wisely, rather than being wasteful.

Match the words to the shape

Abundant, Enable, Risk, Rely, Triumph, Gasp

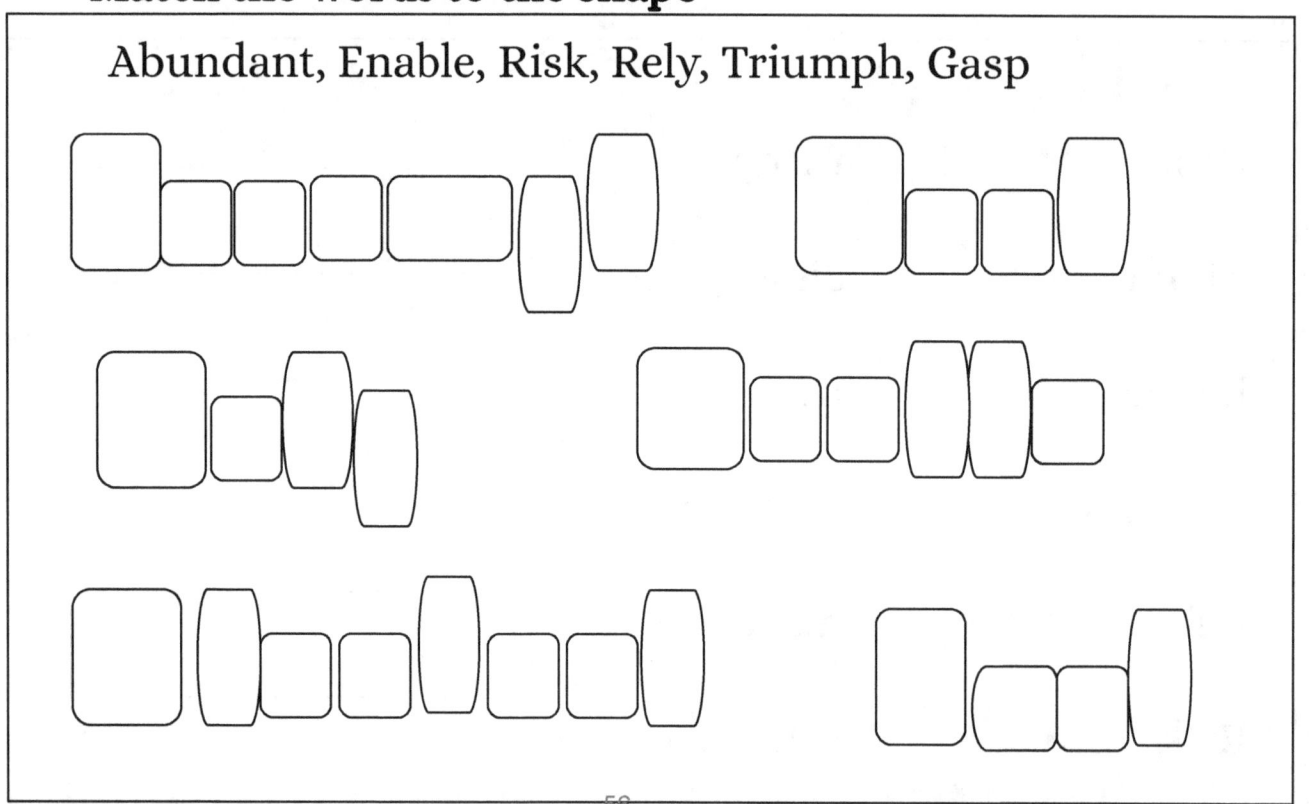

What rhymes with these words

Gasp   _____

Abundant   _____

Enable   _____

Triumph   _____

Rely   _____

Risk   _____

Find hidden words

Gasp   _____

Abundant   _____

Enable   _____

Triumph   _____

Rely   _____

Risk   _____

Identify the synonyms of the words you are practicing in this lesson by circling them.

As I stood atop the mountain, I couldn't help but _____ with wonder at the breathtaking view before me. The rolling hills and _____ forests stretched out as far as the eye could see, a testament to the _____ beauty of nature. I couldn't have made it this far without my strong legs, which _____ me to hike to such heights.

Reaching the summit was a true _____ for me, as it took months of _____ and dedication to get there. I knew that I could always _____ on my own abilities to conquer any challenge, no matter how daunting the _____.

But with great _____ come great _____. As I began the descent, I knew that I had to be careful not to _____ on the loose gravel. The _____ of injury was real, but I knew that I could overcome it by taking small, careful steps and remaining focused.

Answers: Gasp - Inhale sharply/Catch breath, Abundant - Plentiful/Copious
Enable - Empower/Facilitate, Triumph - Victory/Success, Rely - Depend/Count on
Risk - Hazard/Peril

Lesson 7

```
S B A B U N D A N T E N B H O V
E X Q M J R B N N K B X Q P R R
X I H C P V K X Y A Y A Z V J A
A N D K T O Y B Y Z O X R M H D
V R Q B G R G A S P X O A E W J
R P L B U Y I H S R Y C M P L P
Z I G R I S K U G L G P D Y K Y
V L Q O O T K C M Z R V L L U H
W P U V T R Y A Q P Q O I R G N
N K Z R K C D M D H H R X A B Z
E C V D T A X O S F G K C O Q D
Z R H E N A B L E Y P Z T B E Y
O F J Z N K P R J P W S H N C X
D G Q S L O F J I U L L T U D J
Z Z Z F D W R F C D W J T W L F
B B I H B Y R H I Z B H A Q M H
```

ABUNDANT   ENABLE
GASP   RELY
RISK   TRIUMPH

Lesson 8

Re-write Words

Continent			
Doze			
Examine			
Glide			
Suitable			
Value			

Find Letters

Continent	g a p s c e n r o m j n f p e t i p n s e r n m t
Doze	g r o f s b d c q a b r p o t s n t d e z j a o e k
Examine	z e m b c x q a n h o s m a i b t n p l a t i e n
Glide	t k j i r l n g m c a h l i u q m t d c x p u h e g
Suitable	A b s l p u r i a l p t e n g h a q x a b l n c e y t
Value	B p s e v g l w r n e f i a d g f s t d l i k w b u e

Find Meanings from Dictionary and write them here

Continent _____

Doze _____

Examine _____

Glide _____

Suitable _____

Value _____

Write out these words in Capital letters

continent _____

doze _____

examine _____

glide _____

suitable _____

value _____

Across

3. Appropriate or fitting for a particular purpose or situation
4. To move smoothly and effortlessly
6. A landmass that is surrounded by water on all sides

Down

1. To examine or scrutinize something closely
2. To appraise the worth or usefulness of something
5. To sleep lightly or briefly

Fill this passage by using words you are practicing in this lesson

1. The scientist asked me to _____ the test results to see if there were any anomalies.
2. The airline announced that it will be adding new flights to a new _____ starting next month.
3. After a long day of work, I like to _____ on the couch for a little while before getting up to make dinner.
4. The furniture salesman assured us that the couch we picked out was _____ for our living room.
5. My grandmother taught me how to _____ on ice skates when I was a child.
6. When considering whether to buy something, it's important to assess its _____ to determine if it's worth the cost.

Match the words to the shape

Continent, Doze, Examine, Glide, Suitable, Value

What rhymes with these words

Continent   _____

Doze   _____

Examine   _____

Glide   _____

Suitable   _____

Value   _____

Find hidden words

Continent   _____

Doze   _____

Examine   _____

Glide   _____

Suitable   _____

Value   _____

Write out the Synonyms and Antonyms of these words

	Synonyms	Antonyms
Continent		
Doze		
Examine		
Glide		
Suitable		
Value		

Match the Unscramble Words

Continent	lideg	----------------------------------
Doze	eiabutls	----------------------------------
Examine	leavu	----------------------------------
Glide	onntncite	----------------------------------
Suitable	ozde	----------------------------------
Value	iamexne	----------------------------------

Reading Comprehension Practice
Read the passage and answer the questions

The continent of Africa is a vast and diverse landmass with many different regions and cultures. For travelers who are interested in exploring the continent, it's important to examine the different regions and climates to find a suitable itinerary. One of the best ways to see the beauty of Africa is by gliding over it in a hot air balloon, but travelers should also be prepared for long days of hiking and exploring on foot. During breaks, it's essential to doze off and rest to avoid exhaustion.

The value of natural resources on the continent cannot be overstated. From diamonds and gold to oil and gas, Africa is rich in resources that are highly valued around the world. However, it's important to ensure that these resources are extracted in a way that is sustainable and benefits the local communities. Additionally, there is immense value in the cultural diversity of Africa, which includes hundreds of different languages, traditions, and religions.

1. What are some different regions of Africa that travelers might want to examine before planning their trip?

2. Why is it important to doze off and rest during long days of exploration?

3. What are some examples of natural resources that are highly valued on the continent of Africa?

Lesson 8

h	b	d	s	w	a	n	e	o	l	e	x	t	i	f	x
n	z	g	l	e	c	m	g	r	o	c	e	w	g	n	s
a	g	v	r	f	x	n	w	e	w	y	d	l	t	e	y
l	r	p	a	v	s	v	n	b	o	l	b	z	l	o	u
p	i	j	d	g	n	i	y	o	j	c	n	b	f	r	a
r	e	d	o	b	m	v	t	p	j	j	a	d	p	f	u
h	q	l	g	a	m	f	l	h	y	t	d	o	g	s	b
f	a	k	x	y	f	r	c	h	i	o	b	z	x	o	z
h	c	e	j	s	e	k	x	u	d	b	m	e	x	e	p
b	a	y	e	u	u	y	s	h	z	q	v	l	d	b	b
x	t	d	l	i	j	j	z	b	e	u	s	i	b	e	e
b	b	a	h	i	h	v	h	m	x	w	l	v	o	f	h
f	v	r	w	m	h	v	o	t	n	g	c	s	n	k	n
b	r	f	c	o	n	t	i	n	e	n	t	w	w	g	g
u	x	i	x	b	k	m	l	z	z	u	d	k	i	a	g
o	w	s	n	p	j	p	v	e	y	s	o	d	t	m	d

CONTINENT DOZE
EXAMINE GLIDE
SUITABLE VALUE

Lesson 9

Re-write Words

Brief			
Brilliant			
Custom			
Explore			
Habit			
Vision			

Find Letters

Brief	g a b s c e n r c m j i f p e t w p f s o r t n m p
Brilliant	g r o f s b A c r a b i p u l s n l d i d j a o n k t
Custom	z a m b c e q a n h u s r a n b t n p l o j t i e m
Explore	t k j i r e n d m x a h k i p q m l d c o p r h g e
Habit	A b d l h d r i a l p t e n b h s q x i f l n c t y t e
Vision	B p s e v g l w r n e f i a d g f u s t d l i o k w n

Find Meanings from Dictionary and write them here

Brief _____

Brilliant _____

Custom _____

Explore _____

Habit _____

Vision _____

Write out these words in Capital letters

brief _____

brilliant _____

custom _____

explore _____

habit _____

vision _____

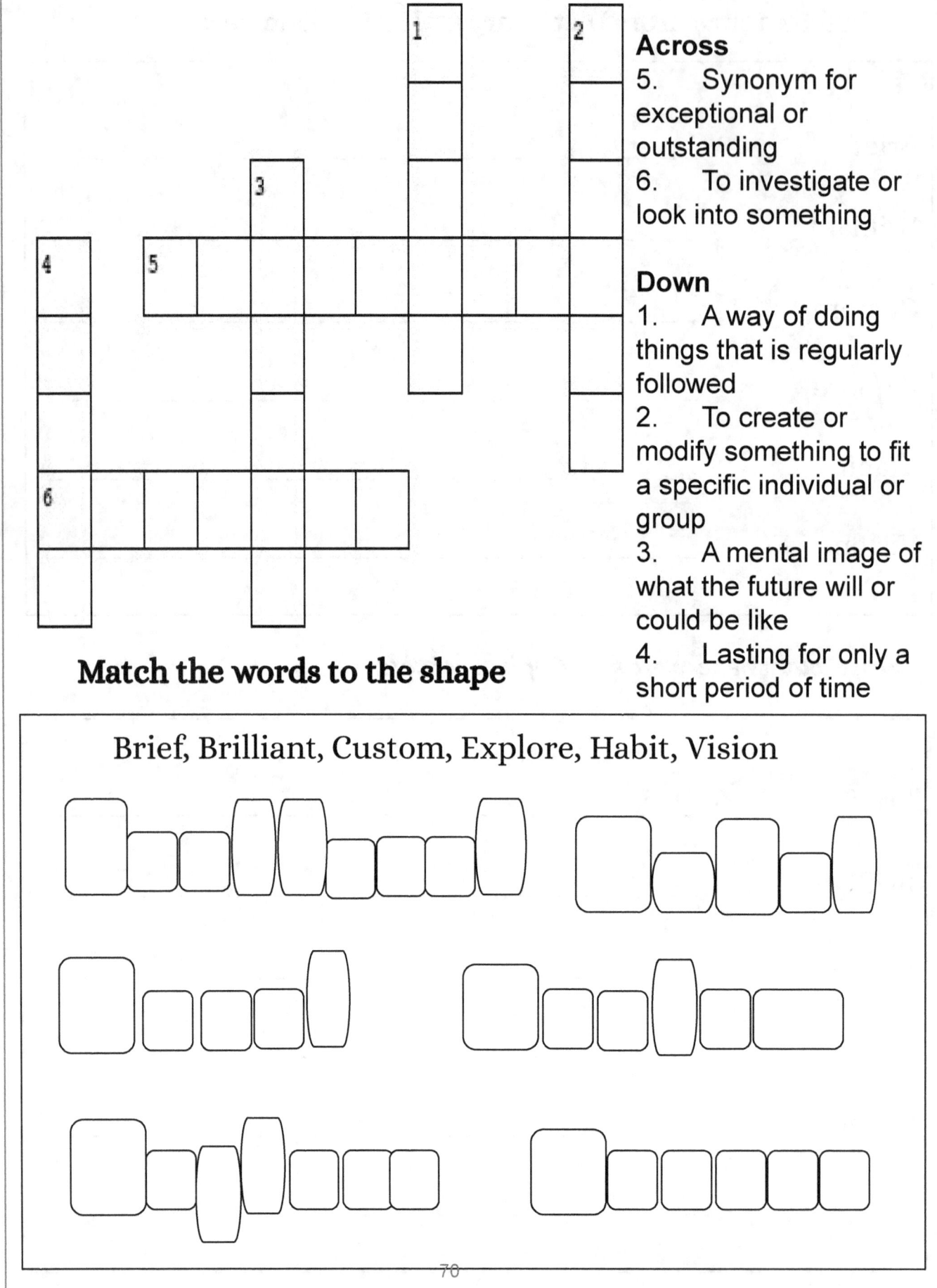

Across
5. Synonym for exceptional or outstanding
6. To investigate or look into something

Down
1. A way of doing things that is regularly followed
2. To create or modify something to fit a specific individual or group
3. A mental image of what the future will or could be like
4. Lasting for only a short period of time

Match the words to the shape

Brief, Brilliant, Custom, Explore, Habit, Vision

What rhymes with these words

Brief   _____

Brilliant   _____

Custom   _____

Explore   _____

Habit   _____

Vision   _____

Find hidden words

Brief   _____

Brilliant   _____

Custom   _____

Explore   _____

Habit   _____

Vision   _____

Write out the Synonyms and Antonyms of these words

	Synonyms	Antonyms
Brief		
Brilliant		
Custom		
Explore		
Habit		
Vision		

Match the Unscramble Words

Brief   onsivi   ------------------------------

Brilliant   aihbt   ------------------------------

Custom   epxroel   ------------------------------

Explore   iefrb   ------------------------------

Habit   tbliniral   ------------------------------

Vision   umscto   ------------------------------

Fill following passage with the words you are practicing in this lesson

To achieve your _____, it's important to develop a daily _____ that aligns with your goals. Take a _____ moment each morning to reflect on your long-term _____ and how you can make progress towards them today. Don't be afraid to _____ new ideas and strategies, and be willing to adapt your approach as needed. Remember that success is a _____ process, not an overnight achievement.

Identify the synonyms of the words you are practicing in this lesson by circling them.

To excel in your goal it's crucial to form a routine that aligns with your mission. Take a quick moment each day to reflect on your long-term objective and how you can move closer to achieving them. Don't be afraid to experiment with new ideas and strategies, and be open to modifying your approach as needed. Remember that success is a exceptional process that requires dedication and hard work.

Lesson 9

```
r i s r g m b t o r j h n q i d
h t k k l b m z r g j u r j b f
y a p s b v e r v m x l e t v e
c f b d z q y o e f t e e q f n
j j h i s l y r u o t v v e a a
g j k m t e o j a n o c i j n w
d v v s b l g q a t s r s e k f
z v d x p w c i m w b m e m c b
e p e x k e l v b u e i p p y u
k u e j r l p n v c u s t o m r
d s o q i w j z k t l r i g w z
j p o r t r h j i z o m w y a l
i y b l z r e i q d e t u i z h
f x x g l b a k k u t j e o r a
c h q z n v x x v i s i o n b u
g c w o j m u c o x h u p c r x
```

BRIEF BRILLIANT
CUSTOM EXPLORE
HABIT VISION

Lesson 10

Re-write Words

Bounce			
Coward			
Diagram			
Globe			
Remark			
Alert			

Find Letters

Bounce	g a b s c o n r u m j f p n t w c f s o e t n m i
Coward	g r o f s b A c r o b i p u l w n l d a d j r n d t i
Diagram	z a m d c i q a n h u s r g a r b t a p l o m t i e
Globe	t k j i r e n g m x a h l i p q m k d c o p r b g e
Remark	A b d l r d r e a l p t e m b h a q x i f r n c k y t
Alert	B p s a v g l w n e f i a d r f u s t d l i o k w n e

Find Meanings from Dictionary and write them here

Bounce   _____

Coward   _____

Diagram   _____

Globe   _____

Remark   _____

Alert   _____

Write out these words in Capital letters

bounce   _____

coward   _____

diagram   _____

globe   _____

remark   _____

alert   _____

Fill in the blanks with the words you have learned in this lesson.

1. The basketball _____d off the rim and back into the player's hands.
2. The _____ refused to confront the bully and instead ran away.
3. The professor drew a _____ on the whiteboard to help explain the complex concept.
4. The astronaut looked down at the blue and green _____ below him.
5. "That's a great idea!" she exclaimed in _____.
6. The tornado warning system issued an _____ to residents to seek shelter immediately.

Match the words to the shape

Bounce, Coward, Diagram, Globe, Remark, Alert

What rhymes with these words

Bounce _____

Coward _____

Diagram _____

Globe _____

Remark _____

Alert _____

Find hidden words

Bounce _____

Coward _____

Diagram _____

Globe _____

Remark _____

Alert _____

Reading Comprehension Practice
Read the passage and answer the questions

The globe is a remarkable invention that has allowed people to understand the world in ways that were once impossible. By looking at a map or a diagram of the world, we can learn about the different continents and countries, as well as the many cultures and languages that exist on our planet. However, it's important to be alert to the fact that not everyone is as curious or brave as we might be. Some people may be too cowardly to venture out into the unknown, and may instead prefer to stay in their own small corner of the world.

But for those who are willing to bounce outside of their comfort zone, the rewards can be immense. Traveling to new places and experiencing different cultures can broaden our understanding of the world and help us to see things from different perspectives. It can also help us to appreciate the things we have in our own lives, and to recognize the commonalities that connect us all.

1. Underline the words that you are practicing in this lesson as well as any other difficult words.

2. What is a globe, and how has it allowed us to understand the world?

3. How can traveling to new places and experiencing different cultures broaden our understanding of the world?

4. In what ways can this help us to appreciate the things we have in our own lives, and to recognize the commonalities that connect us all?

Across
2. A lively rebound
4. A person who lacks courage
6. A warning or notification

Down
1. A written or spoken comment
3. A spherical model of the earth
5. A visual representation of information

Write out the Synonyms and Antonyms of these words

	Synonyms	Antonyms
Bounce		
Coward		
Diagram		
Globe		
Remark		
Alert		

Match the Unscramble Words

Bounce   Earrkm   ----------------------

Coward   trlae   ----------------------

Diagram   cbnoeu   ----------------------

Globe   Irgdaam   ----------------------

Remark   drcoaw   ----------------------

Alert   lebgo   ----------------------

Lesson 10

```
h d j u k e t m d q x k n r f h
j q a j a s d i a g r a m y q e
w n s m g o y k f d f i h d d q
w z m e r n j j z j j a t w p c
p n s x b e l l t i j b r x p l
i i u m r u m r c g w f d z r a
e r s r d i e a d g l o b e a k
p v g p w l r r r s d a s o v h
r v k d a c a f x k l e k q m w
g i v v x w g m r i t n j s y e
u i u q o e a r n w f b b r d w
d g y c t y a s x o c p o b h j
l j q g m v x k i k b s u a i u
v w i y t i x l y h n n m p d
d v l a a o c e e g l g c f h v
x d i q i x e d a b z i e s v k
```

alert
coward
globe

bounce
diagram
remark

Lesson 11

Re-write Words

Avoid			
Deed			
Loyal			
Grace			
Rare			
Respect			

Find Letters

Avoid	m a b s c v n r u m j f p o t w i f s o e d n m
Deed	g r o f s d A c r o b e p u l w e l d a t j r n d t
Loyal	z l m d c i q a n h u s r y a r b t a p l o m t i
Grace	t k j i r e n g m x r h l i a q m k d c o p r g e
Rare	A b d l r d e a l p i e m b h r q x i f r n c k e i
Respect	B p r a v g l e n s f i a p r f u e t d l c o k w t

Find Meanings from Dictionary and write them here

Avoid _____

Deed _____

Loyal _____

Grace _____

Rare _____

Respect _____

Write out these words in Capital letters

avoid _____

deed _____

loyal _____

grace _____

rare _____

respect _____

Fill in the blanks with the antonyms of the words you have learned in this lesson- Disrespect, misdeed, unreliable, unrefined, plentiful, embrace

1. Sarah's _____ caused her to lose the trust of her colleagues.
2. Stephen's _____ to his team caused a lot of damage.
3. John's _____ behavior made it difficult for him to be taken seriously in professional settings.
4. Opportunities like this are _____ if you know where to look.
5. John's _____ for his colleagues made it difficult for him to work with them.
6. I always try to _____ new experiences and avoid playing it safe.

Match the words to the shape

Avoid, Deed, Loyal, Grace, Rare, Respect

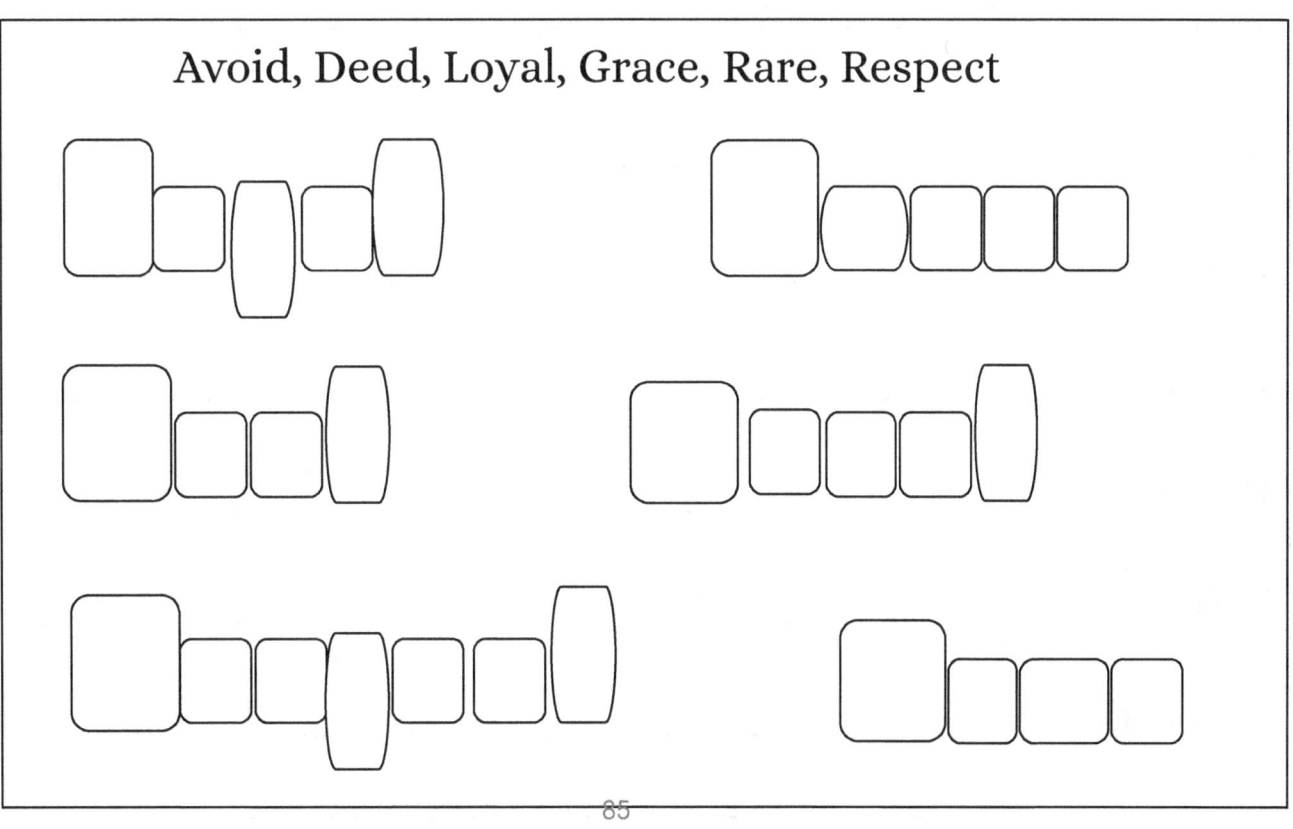

What rhymes with these words

Avoid _____

Deed _____

Loyal _____

Grace _____

Rare _____

Respect _____

Find hidden words

Avoid _____

Deed _____

Loyal _____

Grace _____

Rare _____

Respect _____

Read the passage and fill in the blanks with the words you have learned in this lesson.

As a young adult, Sarah was always taught to _____ risky situations and make responsible decisions. She knew that each _____ she did would have consequences, whether good or bad, and that she was accountable for her actions. Her parents were strict but _____ and supportive, always encouraging her to pursue her dreams and goals.

As Sarah navigated through life, she faced many challenges but always handled them with _____ and composure. She understood that not everyone would agree with her choices, but she stayed true to herself and her beliefs. Her _____ ability to remain calm in stressful situations earned her the respect of her peers and colleagues.

Sarah lived by a code of ethics and principles, treating everyone with respect and kindness. She knew that everyone had a story and that it was important to listen and understand. Her reputation as a fair and just individual allowed her to build strong relationships and networks, both personally and professionally.

Looking back on her life, Sarah was proud of the person she had become. She knew that her success was a result of her hard work, determination, and the values instilled in her from a young age. She hoped to inspire others to live a life of purpose and meaning, one that was guided by love, _____, _____, _____ and a willingness to take responsibility for their actions.

Across

3. Keep away from
5. Elegance and poise

Down

1. Uncommon or unusual
2. Reliable and trustworthy
4. Legal document, Contract or title
6. Honor and regard

Write out the Synonyms and Antonyms of these words

	Synonyms	Antonyms
Avoid		
Deed		
Loyal		
Grace		
Rare		
Respect		

Match the Unscramble Words

Avoid	aercg	_____
Deed	ercpest	_____
Loyal	Rrae	_____
Grace	ivdoa	_____
Rare	edde	_____
Respect	lolya	_____

Lesson 11

```
o f w s y w z w a x x q v m y k
e p f r t n g r a c e r s w j l
i w w o e s k d p e e z r a t l
x m k o r s c c m v i b b i n r
w u n z a z p b a r n e o s z o
h z r y r d h e a f a m l m l x
u f g h e w u o c s d e e d v g
s o v s k u z r q t x a j x x p
a z g m f f k w h z e n h l e h
w v n a h d d i l h e t p y d x
c u o z s y t t b o a u b g v a
p t n i m v g p p f y v o w q t
x p y g d c q f y f k a g v n p
i t w y u i f r n s n z l e u e
i g e a k e n w l y q o z u b k
t f i d y n c z f o d j h k s m
```

AVOID   DEED
GRACE   LOYAL
RARE   RESPECT

Lesson 12

Re-write Words

Attract			
Brave			
Coast			
Journey			
Prevent			
Wander			

Find Letters

Attract	m a b s t v n r t m j f r o t w a f s o c t n m e
Brave	g r o f s b A c r o b a p u l w e l d v t j r e d t
Coast	z l m d c i q o n h u a r y a s b t a p l o m t i
Journey	t k j i r o n g m u r h l i n q m e d c o y r g e
Prevent	A b d p r d e a l p i v m b h e q x i f r n c t e
Wander	B p w a v g l e n s f i a d r f u e t d l c r k w

Find Meanings from Dictionary and write them here

Attract   _____

Brave   _____

Coast   _____

Journey   _____

Prevent   _____

Wander   _____

Write out these words in Capital letters

attract   _____

brave   _____

coast   _____

journey   _____

prevent   _____

wander   _____

Identify the synonyms of the words you are practicing in this lesson by circling them.

1. The new exhibit at the museum is sure to draw in a lot of visitors.
2. We decided to take a drive along the shoreline to enjoy the beautiful views of the ocean.
3. It's important to stop accidents by taking necessary precautions and being aware of potential hazards.
4. Despite the danger, the courageous firefighter rushed into the burning building to save the trapped family.
5. I love to roam through the streets of the city, exploring all of the hidden gems that it has to offer.
6. After much deliberation, we finally embarked on our expedition across the country.

Match the words to the shape

Attract, Brave, Coast, Journey, Prevent, Wander

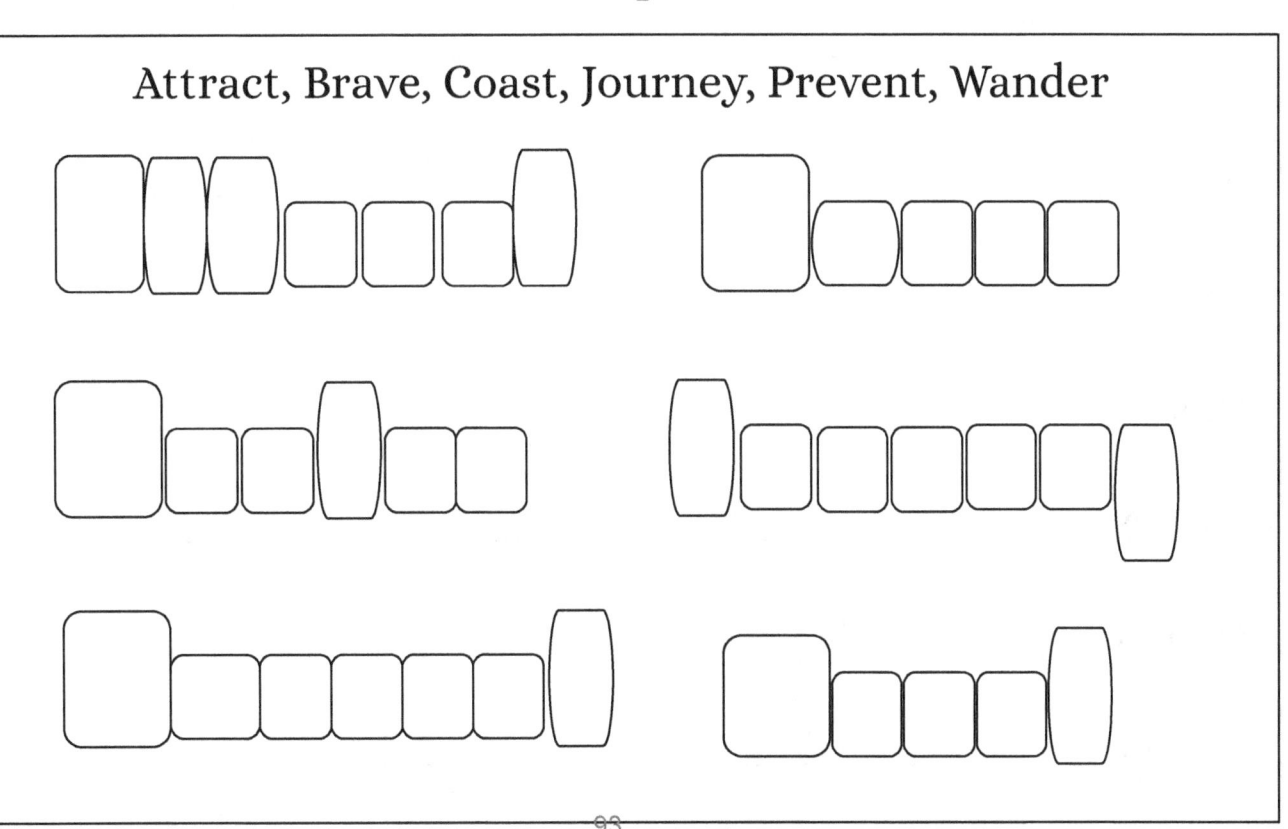

What rhymes with these words

Attract   _____

Brave   _____

Coast   _____

Journey   _____

Prevent   _____

Wander   _____

Find hidden words

Attract   _____

Brave   _____

Coast   _____

Journey   _____

Prevent   _____

Wander   _____

Read the passage and fill in the blanks with the words you have learned in this lesson.

Sarah had always been an adventurous soul. She loved to _____ and explore new places, drawn in by the allure and beauty of the world around her. Her latest _____ had taken her to the coast, where she spent hours walking along the shoreline, taking in the breathtaking views and soaking up the salty ocean air.

As she continued on her _____, Sarah encountered many challenges and obstacles. But she remained_____, drawing upon her inner strength and determination to push forward. She knew that she was capable of overcoming anything that stood in her way, and that each hurdle she faced would make her stronger.

Throughout her travels, Sarah met many interesting people and experienced many different cultures. She had a natural ability to _____ others with her warmth and kindness, and people were drawn to her like moths to a flame. She made many friends along the way, each one adding to the richness and diversity of her life.

But Sarah was also aware of the dangers and risks that came with her adventurous spirit. She took great care to _____ accidents and mishaps, always staying alert and aware of her surroundings. She knew that her love of adventure was not without its risks, and that she needed to be cautious and careful in order to stay safe.

As her latest _____ came to an end, Sarah reflected on all that she had experienced and learned. She realized that life was a journey, full of twists and turns, highs and lows. But as long as she remained _____ and open to new experiences, she knew that she would continue to _____ the beauty and wonder of the world around her.

Across

3. Courageous and fearless
4. Stop or hinder
5. Allure or Appeal to

Down

1. Roam or meander
2. Trip or voyage
6. Shoreline or seashore

Write out the Synonyms and Antonyms of these words

	Synonyms	Antonyms
Attract		
Brave		
Coast		
Journey		
Prevent		
Wander		

Match the Unscramble Words

Attract	veptren	-------------------------------
Brave	dawrne	-------------------------------
Coast	yoenrju	-------------------------------
Journey	stoca	-------------------------------
Prevent	vareb	-------------------------------
Wander	ctatart	-------------------------------

Lesson 12

```
r g l k o q q x y s e u j v v t
o f a w j s a j h x y e j f r t
z n g n a w i p d c x q f u g k
a v e a n n r w k k e p u b f j
z j g o g q d k r t d k p y c o
m p o m a g p e n i q u h b o d
l t r u y j o q r j c b f d d k
d n t e r m x z b r a v e f d b
h w p x v n d i a i o l n g k s
r a v n v e e i u w t m z p v f
s t w j h w n y c j c k c y x y
d p f m d h h t o r r s f x g j
t g s j h p w r a a t t r a c t
n j p i v q m w s p o g f s y b
v q k s q f k m t c q u h h a p
i p g l s x v e h m e g v o e g
```

ATTRACT
COAST
PREVENT

BRAVE
JOURNEY
WANDER

Lesson 13

Re-write Words

Ancestor			
Abrupt			
Humble			
Envy			
Responsible			
Valiant			

Find Letters

Ancestor	m a b n t v c r t m j f e o t w s f t o c t r m e
Abrupt	g r o f s b A c r o b a p r l w e l d u t j p e d t
Humble	z l m h c i q u n h u m r y a s b t a p l e m t i
Envy	t k j i r o n g m e r h l i n q m v d c o y r g e
Responsible	A b d p r d e a l s i p m o n q s i f r b c t l i e
Valiant	B p w a v g l a n s l i a d r f n e t d l c r k w

Find Meanings from Dictionary and write them here

Ancestor _____

Abrupt _____

Humble _____

Envy _____

Responsible _____

Valiant _____

Write out these words in Capital letters

ancestor _____

abrupt _____

humble _____

envy _____

responsible _____

valiant _____

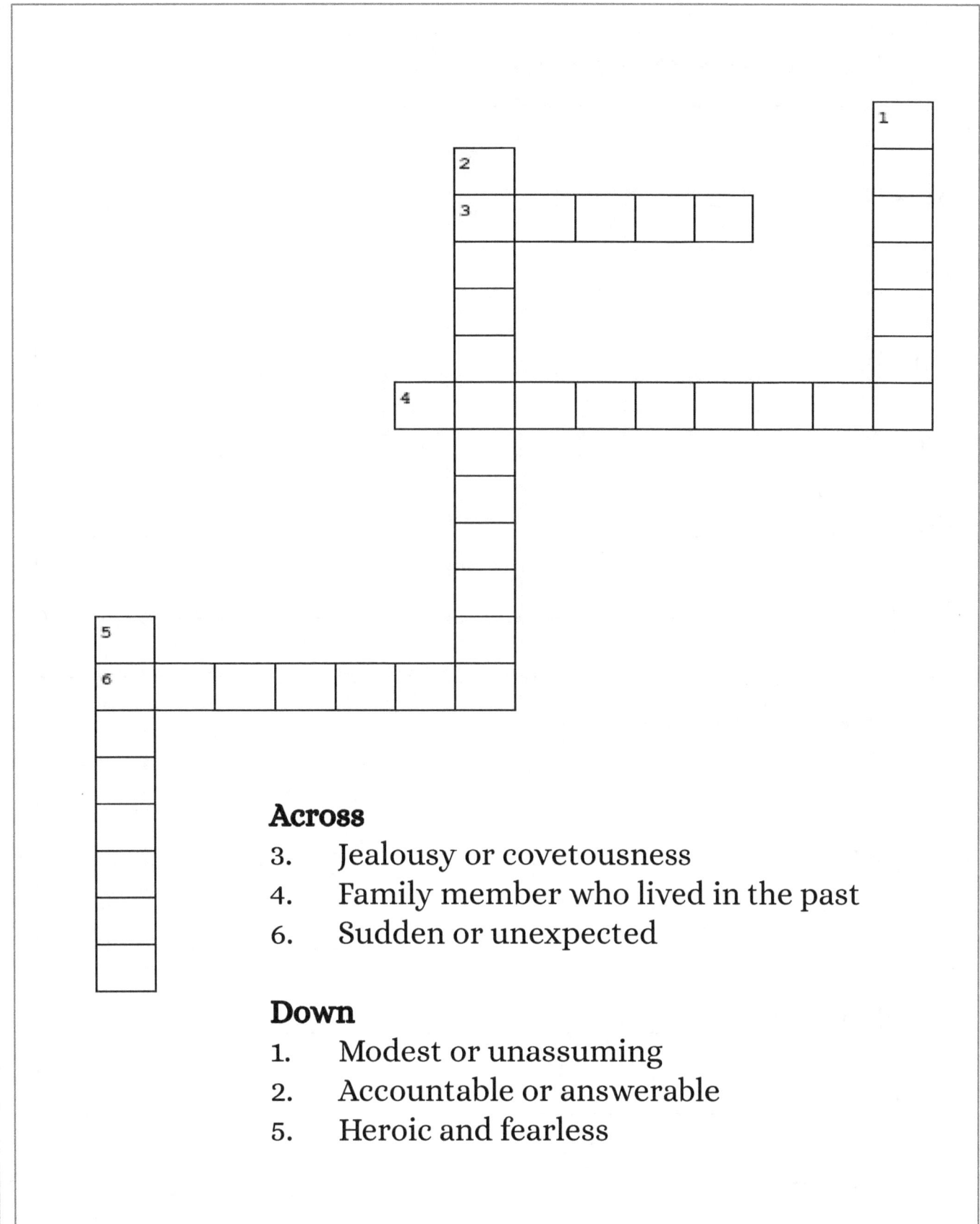

Across

3. Jealousy or covetousness
4. Family member who lived in the past
6. Sudden or unexpected

Down

1. Modest or unassuming
2. Accountable or answerable
5. Heroic and fearless

What rhymes with these words

Ancestor _____

Abrupt _____

Humble _____

Envy _____

Responsible _____

Valiant _____

Find hidden words

Ancestor _____

Abrupt _____

Humble _____

Envy _____

Responsible _____

Valiant _____

Reading Comprehension
underline the words you have learned in this lesson and answers to the questions below

In many cultures, it is common to honor one's ancestors and pay respect to those who came before us. This can be seen in the way that people celebrate holidays and special occasions, and in the traditions that are passed down from generation to generation.

However, sometimes it can be difficult to live up to the high standards set by our ancestors. We may feel like we are not good enough, or that we can never measure up to the accomplishments of those who came before us. This can lead to feelings of inadequacy and even envy towards others who seem to have more success or good fortune.

In these moments, it is important to remember that our ancestors were not perfect. They, too, faced challenges and setbacks, and it is only through their determination and valiant efforts that they were able to achieve greatness. We can learn from their example and strive to live our lives with the same level of courage and determination.

At the same time, it is also important to remain humble and not let our successes go to our heads. We should remember that we are responsible for our own actions and decisions, and that it is only through hard work and dedication that we can achieve our goals.

In the end, our ancestors are an important part of who we are, but they do not define us. It is up to each of us to chart our own path in life and to make the most of the opportunities that come our way. By doing so with courage and humility, we can honor the legacy of those who came before us and pave the way for future generations to come.

1. What is the common practice in many cultures?

2. Who is responsible for our own actions and decisions?

Write out the Synonyms and Antonyms of these words

	Synonyms	Antonyms
Ancestor		
Abrupt		
Humble		
Envy		
Responsible		
Valiant		

Match the Unscramble Words

Ancestor	ltvaani	------------------------------
Abrupt	pnrebeossli	------------------------------
Humble	ncasoret	------------------------------
Envy	rputba	------------------------------
Responsible	lmheub	------------------------------
Valiant	nevy	------------------------------

Complete the following sentences by using synonyms and antonyms of the words you have learned

★ She was _____ about her achievements and didn't like to brag.

★ His _____ attitude made it difficult for others to work with him.

★ The storm came _____ and caught us off guard.

★ The transition from summer to fall is usually _____.

★ She felt a pang of _____ when she saw her friend's new car.

★ Practicing gratitude can help reduce feelings of _____.

★ My _____ immigrated to this country in the early 1900s.

★ I am a _____ of my great-great-grandfather.

★ The manager was _____ for the success or failure of the project.

★ He was fired for being _____ and not showing up to work on time.

★ The firefighters were _____ in their efforts to put out the fire.

★ Running away from a problem is a _____ thing to do.

⟹ **Sudden, Gradual, Jealousy, Contentment, Brave, Cowardly, Forefather, Descendant, Modest, Arrogant, Accountable, Irresponsible,**

Lesson 13

```
d q o e c v c d m c w g u x y x
p q g x g o i c j i c d r o v p
r s s f t t l a g t f z q c u e
d s c x p v s j e c m h w g w u
a a k u f a r g j w r s y t v m
n q r o y l d p b r z g p y c u
m b c i h i h i b y b z t w x r
a e l x b a f m e p p q a r r z
r n c u n n h l h e y s o j v z
j r n z u t v l i o n t p e u q
c g l s o r u v s e s v l v s z
c o w l g k h p e e a b y s b x
l x i r b f s m c x m n h m z c
e b e e b i o n p u h z s p t b
o u o h v j a m h f v f h o a w
o p y c r e s p o n s i b l e b
```

ABRUPT   ANCESTOR
ENVY   HUMBLE
RESPONSIBLE   VALIANT

Write a short story using the words you have learned in this lesson

Match the words to the shape

Ancestor, Abrupt, Humble, Envy, Responsible, Valiant

Lesson 14

Re-write Words

Anticipate			
Appeal			
Essential			
descend			
recognise			
Variety			

Find Letters

Anticipate	m a b n t v i r t c j f i o t p s f a o c t r m e n
Appeal	g r o f s b A c r o b a p r l w e p d e t j p a d l
Essential	z l e h c s q s n h e m n y t s b i a p l e m t i
Descend	t d j e r o s g m c r h l e n q m v d c o y r g
Recognise	A b d p r d e a l c i p m o n g s i n r b i t s i e
Variety	B p w a v g l a n r l i a d e f n e t d l y r k w

Find Meanings from Dictionary and write them here

Anticipate _____

Appeal _____

Essential _____

Descend _____

Recognise _____

Variety _____

Write out these words in Capital letters

anticipate _____

appeal _____

essential _____

descend _____

recognise _____

variety _____

Across
4. Necessary or crucial
5. Identify or acknowledge
6. Attract or interest

Down
1. Assortment or diversity
2. Expect or foresee
3. Go down or drop, Inherit

Write out the Synonyms and Antonyms of these words

	Synonyms	Antonyms
Anticipate		
Appeal		
Essential		
Descend		
Recognise		
Variety		

Match the Unscramble Words

Anticipate	aytvire	_____
Appeal	secrogeni	_____
Essential	lpeapa	_____
Descend	enaitapcti	_____
Recognise	papela	_____
Variety	scenedd	_____

What rhymes with these words

Anticipate _____

Appeal _____

Essential _____

Descend _____

Recognise _____

Variety _____

Find hidden words

Anticipate _____

Appeal _____

Essential _____

Descend _____

Recognise _____

Variety _____

Complete the following passage by using the words you have learned

As the holiday season approaches, many people _____ the festivities and gatherings that come with it. One _____ part of these celebrations is the food, which often includes a _____ of dishes and flavors.

When planning a holiday meal, it is important to take into account the dietary needs and preferences of guests. This can sometimes be a challenge, as some guests may have allergies or other restrictions that limit what they can eat. In these cases, it is important to _____ their needs and make accommodations whenever possible.

Another important consideration when hosting a holiday gathering is the atmosphere. You want to create an environment that is welcoming and comfortable for your guests, and that _____ to their senses. This can include things like decorations, music, and lighting, all of which can contribute to the overall mood of the event.

As the evening winds down and guests begin to _____ upon the dessert table, it is a good time to reflect on the joy and camaraderie that has been shared. By anticipating the needs and preferences of your guests, and creating an atmosphere that _____ their individual tastes, you can ensure that everyone has a memorable and enjoyable experience.

Lesson 14

```
z a r y n j b q c y v i u z k d
d n y d u m u s a j h d r r p x
q t f d m q m k f t u r i x r j
w i v g t z o e r z m e d p h j
h c v j w c o z e x h c e l z r
r i a p n f y h a l b o s q z i
b p r y g u r n t e b g c s f t
j a i q g b l r t s f n e m g o
d t e w b a p s c s d i n h h i
l e t o e l y l v e r s d h u c
c n y p l w d t v n r e a u i n
f l p p j x s u q t n l j n d h
v a j y k v s e m i v e o t i j
t s l p n n d h v a n t p v q l
i i i u m k t c p l v o z o o x
o f t a a w u w r z z w i w p b
```

ANTICIPATE   APPEAL
DESCEND   ESSENTIAL
RECOGNISE   VARIETY

Write a short story using the words you have learned in this lesson

_____
_____
_____
_____
_____
_____
_____
_____
_____
_____
_____
_____
_____
_____
_____

Match the words to the shape

Anticipate, Appeal, Essential, Descend, Recognise, Variety

Lesson 15

Re-write Words

Accelerate			
Content			
Desire			
Impact			
Mock			
Shabby			

Find Letters

Accelerate	m a b c t c i t e j f l o t e r f a o c t r m e n p
Content	g r c f s b a r o b n p r t w e p d e t j p a t l n
Desire	z l d h c s q s n h e m n y t s b i a p l r m t e
Impact	I d j e r o s g m c r h p e n q a v d c o y t g s
Mock	A b d p r m e a l c i p o n g c i n r b i t s i k x
Shabby	B s w a v g h a n r l i a b e f n e d l y r k w

Find Meanings from Dictionary and write them here

Accelerate _____

Content _____

Desire _____

Impact _____

Mock _____

Shabby _____

Write out these words in Capital letters

accelerate _____

content _____

desire _____

impact _____

mock _____

shabby _____

What rhymes with these words

Accelerate _____

Content _____

Desire _____

Impact _____

Mock _____

Shabby _____

Find hidden words

Accelerate _____

Content _____

Desire _____

Impact _____

Mock _____

Shabby _____

Across
1. Strong effect or influence that something has
5. To increase speed or rate of something
6. In poor condition, worn out or untidy in appearance

Down
2. Satisfied and happy with what one has
3. To ridicule or not authentic or real
4. Strong feeling of wanting or wishing for something

Write out the Synonyms and Antonyms of these words

	Synonyms	Antonyms
Accelerate		
Content		
Desire		
Impact		
Mock		
Shabby		

Match the Unscramble Words

Accelerate	comk	-------------------------------
Content	tcmaip	-------------------------------
Desire	bhyasb	-------------------------------
Impact	reesid	-------------------------------
Mock	treececala	-------------------------------
Shabby	ntntcoe	-------------------------------

Complete the following passage by using the words you have learned

In today's fast-paced world, it can be tempting to _____ everything in our lives. We want instant gratification, whether it's in our careers, our relationships, or our personal goals. However, sometimes it's important to slow down and appreciate what we already have. By focusing on the _____ of our lives, we can find more joy and satisfaction in the present moment.

Of course, that doesn't mean we should abandon our _____ for more. Without a sense of _____ and ambition, it can be hard to make progress and achieve our goals. By balancing our desire for growth and improvement with a sense of contentment and gratitude, we can create a more fulfilling and balanced life.

At the same time, we need to be mindful of the _____ of our actions. Even small choices can have a significant impact on the world around us, whether it's in our personal relationships or in the larger community. By avoiding _____ behavior and treating others with kindness and respect, we can create a more positive and supportive environment for everyone.

Finally, it's important to take care of our physical surroundings as well. A _____ or disorganized environment can create stress and distract us from our goals, while a clean and well-maintained space can help us feel more focused and productive. By taking the time to create a supportive and healthy environment, we can set ourselves up for success in all areas of our lives.

In summary, by balancing our desire for growth and improvement with a sense of contentment, being mindful of the impact of our actions, avoiding mocking behavior, and maintaining a clean and organized environment, we can create a fulfilling and successful life.

Lesson 15

h	z	o	q	p	g	n	y	f	b	r	r	s	f	a	q
g	g	m	l	i	d	r	i	d	l	w	f	r	t	n	k
y	x	n	e	m	e	t	t	o	e	m	x	n	y	x	p
h	s	x	q	y	q	j	s	z	i	k	e	x	i	g	l
b	x	v	u	g	t	t	x	e	o	t	f	d	n	m	p
u	a	l	i	k	n	d	y	n	n	l	s	f	a	e	b
p	m	o	n	f	b	o	r	o	f	b	b	j	c	q	y
n	r	f	o	l	q	m	c	c	e	s	t	g	c	m	n
g	w	s	h	a	b	b	y	i	g	p	x	n	e	j	e
e	u	m	z	k	g	a	g	c	p	c	e	k	l	h	g
i	m	p	a	c	t	j	z	w	o	r	c	y	e	q	a
s	u	u	m	s	z	g	b	x	i	o	f	c	r	f	e
z	z	x	d	z	n	v	y	s	m	x	i	r	a	v	p
e	z	i	b	m	l	g	e	r	n	q	q	c	t	j	z
e	z	r	m	n	d	d	t	k	u	q	j	u	e	v	c
u	y	o	n	l	g	m	i	f	b	q	o	y	r	z	y

ACCELERATE   CONTENT
DESIRE   IMPACT
MOCK   SHABBY

Match the words to the shape

Accelerate, Content, Desire, Impact, Mock, Shabby

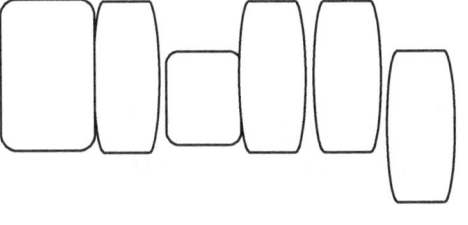
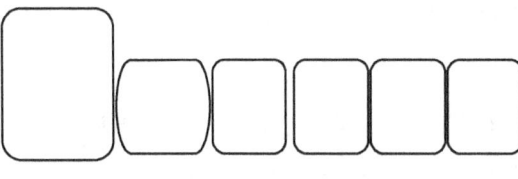
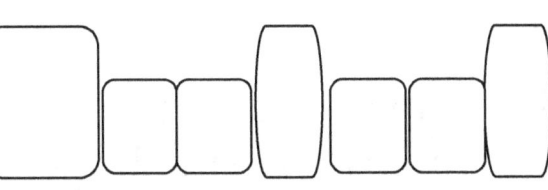
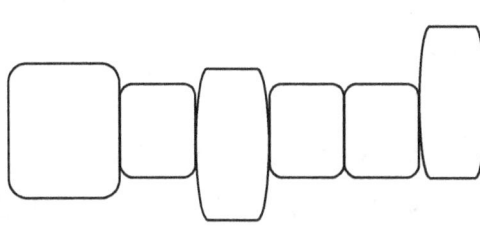
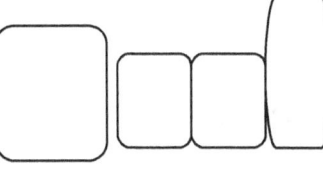
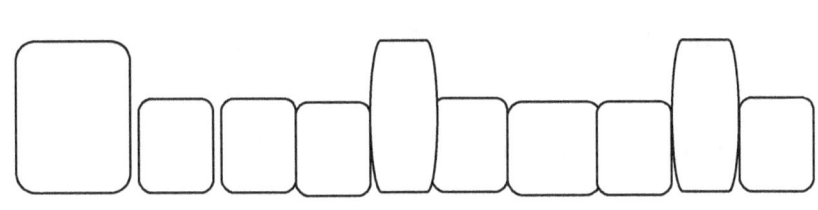

Find and circle the synonyms and antonyms of the words you have learned in this lesson

It's not right to ridicule someone for their appearance or beliefs.
We should praise and encourage our colleagues when they do a good job.

The new policy had a significant effect on the company's profits.
The minor errors in the report had Insignificance on the overall results.

After a long day at work, I'm satisfied with just relaxing at home.
The workers were discontent with their low pay and decided to go on strike.

The old house was in a dilapidated condition and needed major repairs.
She always keeps her workspace neat and organized to stay focused on her tasks.

We need to speed up the production process if we want to meet our deadline.
We should decelerate on the highway if the road conditions are bad.

I have a craving for some ice cream after dinner tonight.
She showed a lot of apathy towards her studies and failed her exams.

Lesson 16

Re-write Words

Dense			
Deposit			
Erupt			
Tragic			
Release			
Vast			

Find Letters

Dense	m a d c t c i t e j f l o t n r f a o s t r m e n
Deposit	g r d f s b a e r p b n o r t w s p d i t j p a t
Erupt	z l e h c r q s n h e u n y t s b i a p l r m t e
Tragic	I t j e r o s g m a r h p e n g a v d i o y t c s
Release	A b d p r m e a l c i p e n g a i n s b i t s e k
Vast	B s w a v g h a n r l i a b s f n e d t y r k w

Find Meanings from Dictionary and write them here

Dense _____

Deposit _____

Erupt _____

Tragic _____

Release _____

Vast _____

Write out these words in Capital letters

dense _____

deposit _____

erupt _____

tragic _____

release _____

vast _____

Across

3. This word means tightly packed together, with little space between the particles.

4. This word describes something that is extremely sad or terrible.

6. You might make this when you put money in the bank, or when minerals settle out of a liquid and form a solid

Down

1. When a volcano does this, it spews lava, ash, and gases into the air.

2. To do this is to set something free, like a bird from a cage or a product from a company.

5. This word means very large in size or extent, like an ocean or a desert.

Write out the Synonyms and Antonyms of these words

	Synonyms	Antonyms
Dense		
Deposit		
Erupt		
Tragic		
Release		
Vast		

Match the Unscramble Words

Dense	lreease	------------------------------------
Deposit	putre	------------------------------------
Erupt	tasv	------------------------------------
Tragic	sende	------------------------------------
Release	tsdeopi	------------------------------------
Vast	rgacti	------------------------------------

What rhymes with these words

Dense _____

Deposit _____

Erupt _____

Tragic _____

Release _____

Vast _____

Find hidden words

Dense _____

Deposit _____

Erupt _____

Tragic _____

Release _____

Vast _____

Lesson 16

x	r	m	j	m	f	p	t	f	s	p	y	x	u	f	s
i	x	i	w	g	x	p	a	t	i	e	f	p	k	a	g
g	a	n	l	q	u	t	o	z	x	d	e	n	s	e	l
o	u	q	l	r	e	w	h	d	y	n	a	z	w	z	r
e	h	p	e	l	c	m	k	u	s	u	f	l	b	m	k
l	p	z	d	u	p	m	r	q	t	m	h	o	g	g	o
a	j	c	e	w	r	i	m	s	t	r	a	g	i	c	q
u	v	c	p	x	q	k	a	g	c	s	p	k	y	q	d
k	v	t	o	u	t	v	c	z	o	r	h	g	c	i	h
b	k	a	s	b	s	s	r	f	a	e	s	o	k	y	d
f	d	s	i	g	w	i	g	d	m	l	e	e	x	s	i
n	o	q	t	c	j	n	a	x	u	e	j	c	a	i	d
w	v	y	i	p	a	j	p	f	w	a	b	r	r	n	c
u	n	w	o	g	f	z	o	q	x	s	k	z	w	g	k
h	s	z	p	x	h	h	p	y	d	e	d	x	c	w	t
q	j	u	v	u	g	t	n	i	q	h	x	r	s	l	

DENSE
ERUPT
TRAGIC

DEPOSIT
RELEASE
VAST

Reading comprehension
Complete the following passage by using the words you have learned and answer the questions

The eruption of Mount St. Helens on May 18, 1980, was a _____ event that forever changed the landscape of Washington state. The blast was so powerful that it caused a massive avalanche of snow, ice, rock, and _____ to flow down the mountain at speeds up to 300 miles per hour. The explosion sent a column of ash and gas more than 15 miles into the sky, creating a dense cloud that blanketed the region for days.

The aftermath of the eruption was devastating. More than 50 people lost their lives, and the surrounding landscape was covered in a thick layer of ash and debris. The _____ ash cloud caused significant damage to crops and livestock, and the once lush forests surrounding the mountain were reduced to a barren wasteland.

Despite the tragedy, the eruption of Mount St. Helens also provided scientists with a unique opportunity to study the impact of volcanic activity on the environment. The _____ amount of data gathered in the years following the eruption has helped researchers better understand the mechanics of volcanic eruptions and develop early warning systems to protect nearby communities.

In addition to the scientific insights, the eruption also had a profound impact on the local economy. The tourist industry saw a surge in visitors eager to witness the aftermath of the explosion, and the release of a documentary film about the eruption helped raise awareness of the power and beauty of the natural world.

Questions:

1. What was the impact of the Mount St. Helens eruption on the landscape?

2. How did the eruption impact the local economy?

3. What did the eruption provide scientists with?

Match the words to the shape

Dense, Deposit, Erupt, Tragic, Release, Vast

Lesson 17

Re-write Words

Crafty			
Flexible			
Indicate			
Noble			
Typical			
Queasy			

Find Letters

Crafty	m a d c t r i t a j f l o t n r f a o s y r m e n
Flexible	g r d f s l a e r p x n o i t w s b d i l j p a t e
Indicate	z l e h n r q d n i e u c y t a b i n p t r m t e
Noble	I t j e n o s g m a r b p e n l a v d i e y t c s
Typical	A b t p r m e y l c i p e n g i n c b a t s e k l
Queasy	B q w u v g e h a n r l i a b s f n e d t y r k

Find Meanings from Dictionary and write them here

Crafty _____

Flexible _____

Indicate _____

Noble _____

Typical _____

Queasy _____

Write out these words in Capital letters

crafty _____

flexible _____

indicate _____

noble _____

typical _____

queasy _____

Across

4. Able to bend easily without breaking
5. Having the characteristics of a particular kind of person or thing
6. Nauseated; feeling sick

Down

1. Having or showing skill in achieving one's ends by deceit or evasion
2. Represent or be a sign of
3. Showing high moral principles and ideals

Lesson 17

```
h  d  e  w  r  l  c  i  b  e  y  e  m  g  e  j
c  z  t  z  c  y  i  a  n  x  k  l  a  w  b  x
m  b  s  y  m  c  p  a  m  d  z  i  t  z  q  c
s  d  s  s  p  t  f  r  c  k  i  d  s  u  g  m
y  w  y  k  h  i  r  r  b  v  m  c  a  h  n  a
t  c  b  c  i  o  c  l  o  a  q  f  a  n  a  r
p  r  o  m  i  y  j  a  l  y  u  t  c  t  j  c
i  n  x  r  t  o  x  f  l  e  e  i  k  x  e  t
g  o  u  f  u  k  v  d  l  k  a  a  n  l  e  d
h  q  a  r  t  m  m  b  j  w  s  u  u  e  h  w
h  r  c  f  z  o  i  e  h  x  y  k  u  e  k  q
c  e  d  r  c  x  j  h  q  g  n  e  r  v  d  j
m  e  j  d  e  k  z  n  o  x  l  s  o  j  e  r
g  v  h  l  o  x  f  a  i  b  j  f  l  z  q  x
q  r  f  l  d  e  x  m  o  l  v  s  f  w  f  v
l  i  k  v  m  j  n  n  a  y  c  b  d  r  g  m
```

CRAFTY   FLEXIBLE
INDICATE   NOBLE
QUEASY   TYPICAL

Write out the Synonyms and Antonyms of these words

	Synonyms	Antonyms
Crafty		
Flexible		
Indicate		
Noble		
Typical		
Queasy		

Match the Unscramble Words

Crafty	yusaqe	----------------
Flexible	Cilypta	----------------
Indicate	lonbe	----------------
Noble	tcfayr	----------------
Typical	ilfxlbee	----------------
Queasy	neidcita	----------------

Complete the following sentences by using the words you have learned

1. He showed a _____ act of kindness by donating all his savings to charity.
2. The _____ fox tricked the other animals to get the food.
3. I felt _____ and dizzy after the bumpy roller coaster ride.
4. Yoga can help make your body more _____ and less prone to injury.
5. The dark clouds _____ that it was going to rain.
6. The behavior of a teenager is _____; they want to be independent but still need guidance.

Match the words to the shape

Crafty, Flexible, Indicate, Noble, Typical, Queasy

What rhymes with these words

Crafty _____

Flexible _____

Indicate _____

Noble _____

Typical _____

Queasy _____

Find hidden words

Crafty _____

Flexible _____

Indicate _____

Noble _____

Typical _____

Queasy _____

Reading comprehension
Complete the following passage by using the synonyms of the words you have learned and answer the questions

The _____ fox, with his sly nature, tricked the other animals into giving him the most food. His _____ approach to problem-solving made him successful in getting what he wanted. However, his behavior was not noble, as he did not share the food with the other animals.

The _____ behavior of the fox, while frowned upon by the other animals, was not out of the ordinary. In fact, it was quite common for animals to exhibit _____ behavior to survive in the wild. While some may see it as a _____ trait to be adaptable and cunning, others may view it as deceitful and untrustworthy.

The fox's behavior indicated that he was not interested in sharing, which made the other animals _____. They felt sickened by the fox's lack of consideration and noble behavior. However, they also acknowledged that in the wild, being flexible and crafty is a necessary trait for survival.

Lesson 18

Re-write Words

Arena			
Inspire			
Orchard			
represent			
Venture			
weary			

Find Letters

Arena	m a d c t r i t e j f l o t n r f a o s y r m e n
Inspire	g r i f s l a n r p x s o i p w s b d i l j r a t e
Orchard	o l e h n r q c n i e h c y t a b i r p t r m d e
Represent	I r j e n o s p m a r b p e n l s v d e y n c t
Venture	A b v p r m e y l c n p e t g u n c b r t s e k
weary	B q w u v g e h a n r l i a b s f n e d t y r k

Find Meanings from Dictionary and write them here

Arena _____

Inspire _____

Orchard _____

Represent _____

Venture _____

weary _____

Write out these words in Capital letters

arena _____

inspire _____

orchard _____

represent _____

venture _____

weary _____

Across

4. To act or speak on behalf of someone or something

5. A piece of land where fruit trees are grown

6. A risky or daring undertaking

Down

1. A place for sports and entertainment events

2. To motivate or give someone an idea

3. Feeling tired or exhausted

Lesson 18

```
A N Q O B E N N B A N U T N L P
N A V R K G P Y K Y R T L C Y D
W N W C I O W M Z W S E U Q J S
L R O H T N U V Y H L M N R Z H
C V E A H A S V E C N B R A H M
P I Z R S R X P L N Y J C E Z K
G O F D A G M K I M T X P D P N
T V O M R U A G W R H U E W Q W
L H X L L E R O G U E B R E R Z
O R S Q C S P B A S P B P E T U
M I A R J O K R U G E Y K X E E
H X B I P W Y J E H X D B N E B
A O R M U E L T J S D V N Q Z B
A E X Z W A G C K A E N P U T M
H D I I A R A T Q N S N K D Y L
H M W O J Y R B S Q A D T X W F
```

ARENA
ORCHARD
VENTURE

INSPIRE
REPRESENT
WEARY

Write out the Synonyms and Antonyms of these words

	Synonyms	Antonyms
Arena		
Inspire		
Orchard		
Represent		
Venture		
weary		

Match the Unscramble Words

Arena	tneervu	------------------
Inspire	crrohda	------------------
Orchard	rayew	------------------
Represent	nseiirp	------------------
Venture	nraae	------------------
weary	serrepnet	------------------

Reading comprehension
Read the passage ; underline the words you have leaned and answer the questions

Arena of Dreams

Sophie always dreamed of being a professional ice skater. She spent most of her free time at the local ice rink, practicing her jumps, spins, and footwork. Despite her natural talent, Sophie knew that becoming a professional skater was no easy feat. She would have to compete against the best of the best at regional and national competitions, and train tirelessly to improve her skills.

One day, Sophie's coach told her about an upcoming competition that would take place at a large arena in the nearby city. The winner of the competition would be offered a spot on the national skating team and a chance to compete at the Olympics.

Sophie was thrilled at the opportunity, but also nervous. The arena was much larger than any rink she had ever skated on before, and the pressure to perform well was intense. However, Sophie was determined to give it her all and represent her town with pride.

The day of the competition arrived, and Sophie stepped out onto the ice to the sound of cheering fans. The arena was packed with spectators from all over the country, and the atmosphere was electric. Despite her nerves, Sophie felt inspired by the energy of the crowd and the thrill of the competition.

Sophie skated her heart out, performing flawlessly and impressing the judges with her talent and passion. When the scores were tallied, Sophie emerged as the winner, earning a spot on the national team and fulfilling her lifelong dream of becoming a professional ice skater.

As she stepped off the ice, Sophie couldn't help but feel a sense of pride and accomplishment. She had taken a risky venture by entering the competition, but her hard work and dedication had paid off. She knew that there would be many more challenges ahead, but for now, she was content to bask in the glory of the arena of her dreams.

Questions:

1. What was Sophie's dream?

2. What did Sophie's coach tell her about?

3. What was Sophie's reaction to the opportunity to compete at the arena?

4. How did Sophie feel during the competition?

Complete the following sentences by using the synonyms of the words you have learned

1. The _____ was filled with enthusiastic fans cheering on their favorite team.
2. Her passion for art always _____d me to pursue my own creative interests.
3. We went apple-picking in the _____ and enjoyed the fresh fruit straight from the trees.
4. As a congressman, it is my duty to _____ my constituents and fight for their rights.
5. Starting a new business is always a risky _____, but with careful planning it can lead to great success.
6. After a long day of hiking, we were _____ and ready for a good night's sleep.

Match the words to the shape

Arena, Inspire, Orchard, Represent, Venture, weary

What rhymes with these words

Arena _____

Inspire _____

Orchard _____

Represent _____

Venture _____

weary _____

Find hidden words

Arena _____

Inspire _____

Orchard _____

Represent _____

Venture _____

weary _____

Lesson 19

Re-write Words

Former			
Destruction			
Threat			
Limp			
Hostile			
Resist			

Find Letters

Former	m a f c t r i t o j f l r t m r f a e s y r m e n
Destruction	d r e f s l a t r p u s o c p t s b d i l j o a t n
Threat	o t e h n r q c n i e h c y t a b i r p t r m d e
Limp	I r l e n o i p m a r b p e n l s v d e y n c t
Hostile	A h v p r m o y l s n p e t g u i c b r l s e k
Resist	B q w r v g e h s n r l i a b s f n e d t y r k

Find Meanings from Dictionary and write them here

Former _____

Destruction _____

Threat _____

Limp _____

Hostile _____

Resist _____

Write out these words in Capital letters

former _____

destruction _____

threat _____

limp _____

hostile _____

resist _____

Across

3. Having been something in the past
5. A statement or action indicating an intention to harm
6. To walk with difficulty, often due to injury or weakness

Down

1. Showing or expressing unfriendliness or opposition
2. The act of causing severe damage or ruin
4. To take action to prevent or oppose something

Write out the Synonyms and Antonyms of these words

	Synonyms	Antonyms
Former		
Destruction		
Threat		
Limp		
Hostile		
Resist		

Match the Unscramble Words

Former	srtise	------------------------
Destruction	haetrt	------------------------
Threat	tlhosie	------------------------
Limp	netrtuscoid	------------------------
Hostile	rmoref	------------------------
Resist	mlip	------------------------

Lesson 19

```
h  c  x  l  c  q  q  t  l  j  a  t  m  i  t  m
u  v  d  k  g  t  s  y  u  p  m  c  g  b  q  k
a  v  p  v  s  i  o  h  n  z  b  h  l  j  t  k
l  x  f  m  s  n  x  e  f  l  y  g  g  k  h  w
i  i  y  e  h  g  q  i  x  o  y  q  i  p  r  k
i  l  r  d  v  o  h  l  i  j  r  d  o  h  e  a
y  f  l  n  e  j  o  q  r  s  j  m  a  l  a  z
z  l  c  u  f  s  s  d  a  u  t  m  e  n  t  d
c  x  v  y  m  b  t  s  f  f  i  j  d  r  a  i
v  j  l  t  k  w  i  r  z  w  f  y  p  s  e  r
z  j  e  m  t  h  l  b  u  m  v  n  e  q  h  p
q  q  z  k  b  o  e  o  m  c  u  x  j  a  u  y
r  m  l  j  i  y  c  f  m  z  t  f  y  j  g  o
l  j  w  i  a  c  g  r  m  h  t  i  m  m  b  a
m  y  p  w  l  i  m  p  t  u  g  t  o  q  d  h
x  f  d  s  f  c  l  w  o  c  t  z  w  n  n  q
```

DESTRUCTION FORMER
HOSTILE LIMP
RESIST THREAT

Reading comprehension
Read the passage ; underline the words you have leaned and answer the questions

The Conservation Effort

The small town of Greenwood had always been proud of its natural beauty, with its lush forests and clear lakes. However, in recent years, the town had faced a growing threat: the destruction of its natural habitats due to logging and mining operations. The once-beautiful forests had been reduced to barren wastelands, and the once-pristine lakes had become polluted and lifeless.

A former resident of Greenwood, Sarah, was dismayed by what she saw when she returned to visit her hometown. She was inspired to take action to preserve the natural beauty of the town for future generations.

Sarah knew that the conservation effort would not be easy. Many people in the town depended on the logging and mining industries for their livelihoods, and were hostile to the idea of change. However, Sarah was determined to resist their opposition and fight for what she believed was right.

Sarah began by organizing a community meeting to discuss the issue. She presented evidence of the negative impact that the logging and mining operations were having on the environment, and proposed alternative sources of income that would not harm the natural habitats of the town.

Despite some initial resistance, Sarah's ideas eventually gained traction. Many people in the town began to realize the importance of preserving the natural beauty of their home, and began to support the conservation effort.

Today, thanks to the hard work and dedication of Sarah and the rest of the community, Greenwood is once again a thriving town, with its forests and lakes restored to their former glory. The former wastelands are now lush orchards and thriving habitats for wildlife. The town has become a shining example of what can be achieved when people come together to resist destruction and protect the beauty of the natural world.

Questions:

1. What was the threat facing the town of Greenwood?

2. What inspired Sarah to take action?

3. Why was the conservation effort not easy?

4. What was Sarah's proposal for alternative sources of income?

What rhymes with these words

Former _____

Destruction _____

Threat _____

Limp _____

Hostile _____

Resist _____

Find hidden words

Former _____

Destruction _____

Threat _____

Limp _____

Hostile _____

Resist _____

Complete the following sentences by using the antonyms of the words you have learned

1. Despite being a _____ champion, John had trouble adjusting to retirement.
2. The _____ caused by the hurricane was devastating to the small coastal town.
3. The promise of a reward was a _____ to motivate the employees to work harder.
4. After his injury healed, Tom was able to walk without a _____.
5. Although they were once enemies, the two nations are now _____ and working together.
6. Even though she was tempted to give up, Sarah decided to _____ the urge and keep working towards her goal.

Match the words to the shape

Former, Destruction, Threat, Limp, Hostile, Resist

Lesson 20

Re-write Words

Blend			
Coax			
Fragile			
Instant			
Peculiar			
Response			

Find Letters

Blend	m a f b t r i l o j f l e t m r f a n s y r m e d
Coax	d r e f s c a t r p u s o c p t s b a i l j o x t n
Fragile	f t e h n r q c n a e h c g t a b i r p l r m d e
Instant	I r l e n o i p m a r s b t a n l s v d e y n t c
Peculiar	A h v p r m e y l c n p u l g u i c b a l s r k
Response	B q w r v g e h s n r p i a b o f n e d s y e k

Find Meanings from Dictionary and write them here

Blend _____

Coax _____

Fragile _____

Instant _____

Peculiar _____

Response _____

Write out these words in Capital letters

blend _____

coax _____

fragile _____

instant _____

peculiar _____

response _____

Write out the Synonyms and Antonyms of these words

	Synonyms	Antonyms
Blend		
Coax		
Fragile		
Instant		
Peculiar		
Response		

Match the Unscramble Words

Blend	tsntina	------------------------
Coax	rssneeop	------------------------
Fragile	cuielpra	------------------------
Instant	denbl	------------------------
Peculiar	lreifga	------------------------
Response	axco	------------------------

Down

2. Unusual or distinctive, especially in a way that is interesting or curious

Across

Across
1. A reaction to something that has been said or done
3. To persuade someone to do something through gentle urging or flattery
4. To mix or combine different substances together thoroughly
5. Easily broken, damaged, or destroyed
6. Happening or done immediately, without any delay

What rhymes with these words

Blend _____

Coax _____

Fragile _____

Instant _____

Peculiar _____

Response _____

Find hidden words

Blend _____

Coax _____

Fragile _____

Instant _____

Peculiar _____

Response _____

Lesson 20

n	y	z	y	k	a	q	z	s	j	l	b	l	e	n	d
w	h	c	o	a	x	z	j	b	q	b	t	s	e	y	l
l	h	a	d	m	j	d	d	h	b	r	n	m	l	r	n
w	e	u	c	h	i	w	p	w	q	o	n	o	v	y	d
f	b	c	l	w	q	r	q	h	p	u	k	f	u	b	w
y	j	z	b	n	v	r	l	s	i	n	s	t	a	n	t
s	f	h	c	e	u	r	e	g	b	y	w	p	j	k	l
f	g	f	l	p	e	r	q	p	e	c	u	l	i	a	r
z	x	u	j	p	i	n	d	k	l	u	e	c	c	j	d
e	e	f	v	a	d	o	k	d	a	x	a	o	e	d	b
q	y	z	r	z	b	a	r	q	q	e	m	a	f	q	i
l	u	u	r	a	k	w	y	c	l	i	l	p	r	r	m
p	b	z	b	h	g	z	y	q	l	v	p	p	y	z	u
u	x	k	p	w	f	i	q	c	p	l	o	p	o	y	f
h	r	v	m	i	a	k	l	w	b	j	c	l	t	x	c
y	f	c	j	u	t	h	b	e	p	p	s	v	d	e	q

BLEND   COAX
FRAGILE   INSTANT
PECULIAR   RESPONSE

Apply your knowledge of the words you've learned by completing the following sentences.

1. The company's _____ to the customer's complaint was quick and helpful.
2. With modern technology, we can get _____ access to information from all over the world.
3. She tried to _____ her cat out of the tree with a can of tuna.
4. The new student had a _____ accent that no one else in the class could place.
5. The chef used a _____ of spices to create a unique flavor for the dish.
6. Be careful with that vase, it's very _____.

Match the words to the shape

Blend, Coax, Fragile, Instant, Peculiar Response

We hope that you enjoyed our efforts in creating this spelling workbook. If possible, we would greatly appreciate it if you could provide a review to help us improve future spelling book series.
Your feedback is valuable to us and will allow us to continue creating helpful resources for children.
Thank you in advance for your time and consideration.

For more Publication; visit our website
www.newbeepublication.com

www.ingramcontent.com/pod-product-compliance
Lightning Source LLC
Chambersburg PA
CBHW081617100526
44590CB00021B/3485